Ministry of Culture, Government of the State of São Paulo, through the Secretariat of Culture, Creative Economy and Industry, Municipal Secretariat of Culture and Creative Economy of the City of São Paulo, Fundação Bienal de São Paulo and Itaú present

Not All Travellers Walk Roads

36th Bienal de São Paulo

Of Humanity as Practice

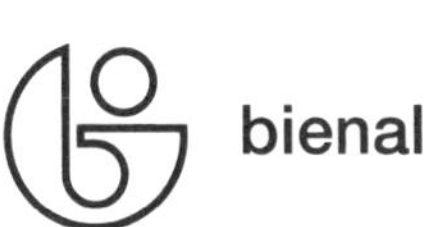

Browse our YouTube channel and check out the documentation of the *Invocation #1*.

Educational Publication

Vol. 1

Souffles:

On Deep Listening and Active Reception

Since 1953, the year of its second edition, the Bienal de São Paulo has stood out for its educational commitment, promoting initiatives that facilitate access to exhibition content for diverse audiences – including teachers, students, and educators. In 2009, the Fundação Bienal established a permanent education team that has since been developing and implementing educational projects for each edition. These projects include publications, guided visits, workshops, and training programs for teachers and educators, all aimed at fulfilling the Fundação Bienal's mission of expanding access to contemporary art.

For the 36th Bienal de São Paulo – *Not All Travellers Walk Roads – Of Humanity as Practice*, the Fundação presents a series of four educational publications with two complementary objectives, both of fundamental importance to the Bienal. The first is to document and share the contributions of the *Invocations* – curatorial gatherings with artists and poets that explore notions of humanity, the exhibition's central theme, through the lens of four distinct geographies: Marrakech, Guadeloupe, Zanzibar, and Tokyo. The second objective is to support the educational project of the 36th Bienal, with these books serving as key resources in the training of mediators and in outreach activities, both during the months of preparation and execution of the exhibition and throughout the traveling exhibitions program that will follow.

As is characteristic of the Bienal de São Paulo, the content of these publications weaves together local and global perspectives, addressing contemporary practices and issues. The result of a partnership with the Center for Art, Research and Alliances (CARA), which co-edited the books with the Fundação Bienal, and the A&L Berg Foundation, which supported the project from the outset, these educational publications are now available in English and will be distributed internationally for the first time, expanding the reach of the Invocations and our educational content, and reaffirming the Bienal's international vocation, which has been continuously enacted for over seventy years.

Andrea Pinheiro
President – Fundação Bienal de São Paulo

CARA is thrilled to co-produce this publication with the Bienal de São Paulo, reinforcing our shared commitment to expanding spaces for artistic and intellectual inquiry. The *Invocations* programs and these four educational volumes echo CARA's dedication to publishing as an act of transformation – where knowledge is not just recorded but activated through encounters across disciplines and geographies. Our institutional approach fosters open-ended research, challenges fixed narratives, and embraces storytelling as a means of keeping ideas in motion, unsettling dominant histories, and opening pathways for unlearning.

Building on this ethos, CARA's publishing program amplifies overlooked voices, supporting elder and mid-career practitioners and alternative historiographies. Our books embrace literary and poetic practices; visual, moving-image, and performance art; and radical action as entangled forces shaping how we understand our interconnected worlds. Through the *Invocations* series, CARA furthers its commitment to publishing as a space of resonance – where artistic and intellectual work resists singular narratives. This collaboration with the 36th Bienal de São Paulo strengthens our mission to amplify artists, scholars, and cultural workers whose contributions shape critical discourse, foster new connections, and expand the boundaries of thought.

At CARA, we ask: How can we dream not only about ourselves? This question guides our editorial vision, inviting us to create spaces where knowledge is shared and deepened in dynamic relation. For us, publishing is a process of bringing into generative constellation – where voices converge, entangle, and expand what can be imagined together. This collaboration embodies that ethos, offering books that challenge, unsettle, and inspire new ways of thinking and being in the world.

Manuela Moscoso
Executive and Artistic Director – CARA

The A&L Berg Foundation, founded in 2023 by Allison and Larry Berg, provides access, tools and resources to create, evolve and sustain diverse perspectives and narratives in the United States visual arts. We support and empower individuals committed to making systemic and scalable impact in their practices and communities.

The Foundation's core program is the ESAP Fellowship, which supports and empowers early stage visual arts curators, educators and administrators working in United States arts spaces and institutions. Through building a long-lasting peer support system, and providing navigational tools and opportunities to create expanded professional networks and communities, the Foundation creates equitable visual arts career pathways and ultimately aims to strengthen and diversify the internal ecosystems of United States art institutions.

Our programs provide access to networks, professional development workshops, international research travel, mentorship, relational and soft skills coaching, and financial support for navigating systemic inequities. Each year, a different jury of esteemed arts professionals nominates candidates based on an agreed upon set of criteria, and we invite six of those individuals to participate in the fellowship cohort. Our guest program director, an arts professional who has already successfully navigated the challenges facing the respective cohort, designs the annual program details with a focus on the relational skills that specific cohort requires for career growth.

During the ten-month fellowship, the Foundation provides five empowerment prongs: mentorship with a more established arts professional; relational skills workshops with specialists spanning a variety of industries; an unrestricted financial grant; a robust international research trip opening doors and offering engagement with visual art leaders and peers from every part of the global art ecosystem and ongoing support for professional growth.

A&L Berg Foundation

The Fundação Bienal de São Paulo thanks its partners CARA and A&L Berg Foundation for their special collaboration on the educational publications of the 36th Bienal.

The Federal Government, through the Ministry of Culture, is celebrating the 36th Bienal de São Paulo in partnership with the Fundação Bienal de São Paulo. Just like the great film festivals, the Bienal de São Paulo – the second oldest art biennial in the world – raises enormous expectations on the global exhibition circuit. This year, with the title *Not All Travellers Walk Roads – Of Humanity as Practice*, inspired by a poem by the renowned Brazilian writer Conceição Evaristo, the Bienal reaffirms its vocation as a major showcase for the most current production on the national and global art scene, without losing sight of its wide-ranging educational activities in the formation of new and well-known audiences.

The Ministry of Culture has been working to strengthen the cultural sector through various initiatives and promotion tools. Policies such as the Paulo Gustavo Law and the Aldir Blanc National Policy for the Promotion of Culture encourage other artistic languages, creating opportunities for artists, cultural producers, managers, and visitors. Creating solid conditions for culture means strengthening the creative economy and encouraging the implementation of perennial, permanent, and democratic cultural policies.

Being alongside projects like the Bienal's new movie theater is a source of pride, as it brings together two issues dear to the government: expanding democratic access to cultural facilities combined with an educational arm capable of mediating and making sense of what is on display. By providing free film screenings accompanied by educational activities, another stage is created to strengthen the culture of our country's award-winning and increasingly active audiovisual field.

The Federal Government remains committed to arts and education, which are indispensable fronts for ensuring the right to citizenship and a fairer future for all. We will continue to invest in initiatives that encourage cultural creation and innovation, ensuring that events such as the Bienal de São Paulo continue to inspire and transform generations.

Margareth Menezes
Minister of Culture – Federal Government of Brazil

For more than 35 years, Itaú Cultural (IC) has played a fundamental role in boosting the appreciation of art, culture and education in a complex and heterogeneous society like Brazil. This role is expanded through essential partners for the development of the cultural and creative economy, such as the Fundação Bienal de São Paulo.

Itaú Unibanco is proud to be a sponsor of the Fundação Bienal de São Paulo – it has been for the past 27 years, with this being the 12th edition held in that period – reaffirming its commitment to promoting the visual arts and their transformative role. The Bienal de São Paulo is an important meeting and exchange space for artists, curators, critics, and the public.

In this field, Itaú Cultural organizes actions for enjoyment, education and promotion, including solo and group exhibitions that take place both at its headquarters on Avenida Paulista, 149 (with free admission) and at venues in Brazil's five regions. Highlights of the 2025 exhibitions include *Carlos Zilio – A querela do Brasil*, curated by Paulo Miyada, which will present a retrospective of this artist who, with erudition and irreverence, explored the tensions of Brazilian art. Exhibitions will also be dedicated to the visual artist Rivane Neuenschwander and the curator and critic Paulo Herkenhoff.

Visit itaucultural.org.br to browse the *Filmes e vídeos de artistas* virtual exhibitions, with experimental audiovisual works, and *Livros de artista na Coleção Itaú Cultural*, whose immersive and interactive features allow for detailed appreciation. At Enciclopédia Itaú Cultural (enciclopedia. itaucultural.org.br) you can access hundreds of entries on figures, works, and events in the visual arts.

Being present at the Bienal de São Paulo reinforces our goal of building links with different audiences, valuing the diversity of formats, thoughts, and subjectivities, and fostering creative and critical thinking through Brazilian art and culture.

Itaú Cultural

Bloomberg is proud to sponsor of the 36th edition of the Bienal de São Paulo. For more than a decade we have supported the Bienal's exceptional contemporary art exhibitions in the stunning Ciccillo Matarazzo Pavilion in Ibirapuera Park and around Brazil, through our partnership with Fundação Bienal. This year's edition continues the tradition of presenting captivating and thought-provoking art installations that are free and open to the public.

Every day, Bloomberg connects influential decision makers to a dynamic network of information, people, and ideas. With more than 19,000 employees in 176 offices, Bloomberg delivers business and financial information, news and insight around the world. Our dedication to innovation and new ideas extends to our longstanding support of arts, which we believe are a valuable way to engage citizens and strengthen communities. Through our funding, we help increase access to culture and empower artists and cultural organizations to reach broader audiences.

Bloomberg

For Bradesco, a Brazilian bank *par excellence* that has just celebrated its 83rd anniversary, art and culture are not only fundamental elements in the formation of a people's identity or the construction of their intangible heritage, but also a journey of inclusion and citizenship, a healthy convergence of different points of view. It is, so to speak, a journey towards the new, but with the care to value what is special enough to be history or tradition.

Therefore, when it comes to art and culture, the boundaries between past, present, and future, between form and content, become meaningless. Everything becomes reflection and learning, everything becomes provocation and surprise.

It was on the basis of this interpretation, combined with the positive view of the role of companies in making possible what society considers important, that Bradesco became a sponsor of the 36th edition of the Bienal de São Paulo, undoubtedly one of the most important events in the country aimed at promoting the arts scene, publicizing the various expressions of art and promoting cultural exchange, with all the good that this brings.

By participating in something that is both great and multifaceted, Bradesco shares with the Fundação Bienal de São Paulo – which has organized the event for more than six decades – the goal of democratizing access to culture, multiplying its reach and promoting the appreciation of art.

It's a path with no end, no turning back, full of challenges and at least one certainty: the more people who take part, the better!

Bradesco

Petrobras has a history of more than forty years of continuously believing in culture as a transformational element and a source of energy for society. By supporting unique projects and long-term partnerships, we have built a relationship of respect and collaboration with producers and initiatives all over the country.

The Petrobras Cultural Program has Brazilianness as its guiding element, which is materialized in the themes, origins, curatorship, history, and characteristics of each project we select. By supporting different projects, we put into practice our belief that culture is an important energy that transforms society. We believe that through creativity and inspiration we promote growth and change.

The Bienal de São Paulo is one of the sector's most prestigious events in the country and the world. Petrobras's sponsorship reinforces the company's role in promoting culture in its various forms, consolidating its position as one of the biggest supporters of the arts in Brazil.

Events such as the Bienal de São Paulo make a significant contribution to the economy, promoting innovation, creativity, and sustainability in the economic dynamic. Petrobras is an ally of Brazil's development in its various sectors. It invests in many forms of energy, and culture is certainly one of them.

Petrobras is proud to support Brazilian culture in its plurality of manifestations, taking art to all audiences, all over the country. Because culture is also our energy.

To find out more about the Petrobras Cultural Program, visit petrobras.com.br/cultura.

Petrobras

Instituto Vale Cultural believes in the transformative power of culture. As one of the main supporters of culture in Brazil, it sponsors and promotes projects that foster connections between people, initiatives, and territories. Its commitment is to make culture increasingly accessible and diverse, while also contributing to the strengthening of the creative economy.

It is therefore a pleasure to be part of the realization of this 36th Bienal de São Paulo and its educational program, which explores new formats and approaches. Developed from the *Invocations* proposed by the curatorial team – encounters with poetry, music, performance, and debates that explore notions of humanity across different geographies – the educational program expands the Bienal's communication with diverse audiences and extends its reach beyond the exhibition space and timeframe, in an interdisciplinary way.

With each new edition, the Bienal invites us to rethink art as an exercise in dialogue, in openness to new narratives, and as a space for learning. In this sense, it aligns with the purpose of the Instituto Cultural Vale: to expand opportunities for learning, reflection, new perspectives, and the sharing of art, culture, and education – both inside and outside museums, throughout Brazil.

Where there is culture, Vale is there

Instituto Cultural Vale

For 110 years, Citi has been part of Brazil's history, accompanying its transformations and driving its development. Our journey is intertwined with that of the country: we are both witnesses to and participants in a Brazil that constantly reinvents itself and moves forward.

More than a financial institution, we believe in the power of culture and education as engines for a more inclusive, innovative, and sustainable future. Investing in these pillars also means celebrating the diversity, creativity, and talent that define the Brazilian spirit.

With this commitment, we are proud, for the first time, to support the 36th Bienal de São Paulo – one of the most important spaces for artistic expression in Latin America, where Brazil thinks, feels, and reinvents itself through art.

We believe in art as an agent of social transformation. Artistic creation has the power to spark dialogue, expand horizons, and inspire new possibilities for the world. By sponsoring the Bienal, we reaffirm our commitment to culture, innovation, and all those who, through art, are building new narratives for both the present and the future.

Citi

Vivo believes in culture as a means of social transformation and is one of the most important brands supporting the visual and performing arts and music in Brazil. Art, like technology, creates connections between people and encourages the search for balance between history, nature and time.

Vivo is currently a sponsor of the most important museums in Brazil, such as the Museu de Arte de São Paulo Assis Chateaubriand (MASP), the Pinacoteca de São Paulo, the Museu da Imagem e do Som (MIS-São Paulo), the Museu Afro Brasil Emanoel Araujo, the Museu de Arte Moderna de São Paulo (MAM SP), as well as the Instituto Inhotim and the Palácio das Artes, both in Minas Gerais, and the Museu Oscar Niemeyer, in Paraná.

Teatro Vivo, located in São Paulo, offers a curated selection of contemporary plays that promote reflection on current issues and value cultural diversity. In addition, it is a fully accessible space, offering resources such as translation into Libras (Brazilian sign language), audio descriptions and trained staff, ensuring inclusion for people with disabilities and reduced mobility. In 2024, it welcomed over 50,000 people.

The brand also supports projects in the world of music that are genuinely Brazilian and regional, reinforcing its proximity with local culture at iconic and traditional events in our country, such as the Parintins Festival, Galo da Madrugada, the Çairé Festival, Lollapalooza, The Town, and Vivo Música.

The brand's initiatives in the cultural sphere broaden access to knowledge with new ways of experiencing and learning, strengthened by the aspects of diversity, sustainability, inclusion and education. All information is gathered and shared on the @vivo.cultura and @vivo Instagram profiles.

Vivo

Confronted with the incessant problems of humanity, perhaps it is worth dwelling a little longer on some open questions, taking sustenance from resources that allow us to dig and build answers procedurally. In this sense, art, in its many guises, offers fertile ground for critical elaborations about the world and ourselves.

The meeting of art and education – both understood as fields of knowledge – enables the torsion of time and space: it becomes possible, thus, to suspend neutralities and dilate what is precipitated in structures. How far is this approach able to infer the real and interfere in it? It allows us to (re)populate imaginaries, to unpick the universalizing statute attributed to concepts, practices and people, and thus to carve out reality with narratives that articulate the individual and the collective, in a procedural and coherent manner regarding the issues that permeate existence.

It is according to this panorama that Sesc São Paulo and the Fundação Bienal, through the 35th Bienal de São Paulo, reiterate their long-standing partnership, a mutual commitment to fostering experiences of coexistence with the visual arts, expanding access to cultural actions and the exercise of otherness.

This partnership, which has been established and renewed for over a decade, has led to the promotion of projects such as simultaneous exhibitions, public meetings, seminars and training for educators, as well as the consolidated itinerant exhibition with excerpts from the Bienal in Sesc units in the wider state of São Paulo. The confluence of choices and propositions is part of the institutional perspective of culture as a right, and conceives, together with one of the largest exhibitions in the country, an accessible horizon for contemporary art in Brazil.

Sesc São Paulo

Foreword

Fundação Bienal de São Paulo

This book is an extension of the investigations into notions of humanity in different parts of the world, engaging with the ideas of the 36th Bienal de São Paulo – *Not All Travellers Walk Roads – Of Humanity as Practice* from the first of the *Invocations, Souffles: On Deep Listening and Active Reception*, which took place in Marrakech in November 2024.

The *Invocations* are meetings with presentations of poetry, research, music, and dance that precede the exhibition in São Paulo. In addition to the one held in Marrakech, others were also held in three other territories: Guadeloupe in December 2024, and Zanzibar and Tokyo, in February and April 2025, respectively.

The edition of this publication is based on the idea of listening to and telling stories as a tool for learning and confronting ongoing processes of dehumanization in the world. Thinking about the 36th Bienal de São Paulo involves the metaphor of the estuary – one of the curatorial concepts guiding the event – as a space of coexistence, of encounter. Co-curator Thiago de Paula Souza instigates us with a question: "What if the Capibaribe River met Tokyo Bay?"

Expanding on the question that arises from this estuary, and in view of the multiplicity of content assembled here, we rehearse a further reflection: what if different educational investigations related to the territory of Brazil encountered those mobilized in Marrakech? What if Gnawa music[1] met a samba *roda*?

23

The *Halqa* and the *Roda*: Listening and Transmitting

In the context of Moroccan culture and North African culture more broadly, *Halqa* designates a singular space. In a translation from Arabic, *Halqa* means "circle" and refers to how people gather in places such as Jemaa el-Fna square in Marrakech, where music, dance, and storytelling gatherings have taken place for centuries, promoting entertainment and education in public space. In the context of *Invocation #1*, *Halqa* also speaks to the notion of an estuary, a living environment that is home to community bonds, art, education, and culture – it is a meeting between the river and the sea, which welcomes and nurtures different forms of life.

This publication also presents itself as a *Halqa* or, to speak to the Afro-Brazilian tradition, a *roda*. This is where words, gestures, and melodies circulate and can be heard, learned, and reproduced like the refrain of a samba that is constantly repeated and recreated in different languages, tones, and accents. They are songs and tales that invoke colors, smells, landscapes, and memories.

Fatima-Zahra Lakrissa's essay tells how, in the 1960s, Farid Belkahia, Mohamed Melehi, and Mohammed Chabâa, from the Casablanca School of Fine Arts, led the art education reform in Morocco's post-independence period. And, alongside theorists such as Toni Maraini and Bert Flint, played a central role in the creation of the *Maghreb Art* magazine (1965–1969), which established methodological and theoretical principles for the revival of traditional and popular arts in Morocco. Through these initiatives, they not only transformed the arts curriculum but also expanded their work beyond the aesthetic plane, reaffirming their connection with society.

This story resonates with Amina Agueznay. She is one of the artists at the 36th Bienal and the daughter of Malika Agueznay, a leading figure in the movement around the Casablanca School of Fine Arts, as well as being recognized as the first woman to develop abstract painting in her country. Amina, who has been creating with artisans in different parts of the world for decades, approaches the relationship between manual labor and the act of listening and telling stories, as well as the value of listening, exchange, and the legacy of her mother and other figures from the Casablanca School, such as Farid Belkahia and Mohamed Melehi, from an affective point of view.

It is also from the point of view of affect and involvement in collective practices that Alberto Pitta speaks. This artist has a special appreciation for the poetics of fabrics and a career spanning over four decades. He is the author of prints featured in afro and afoxé

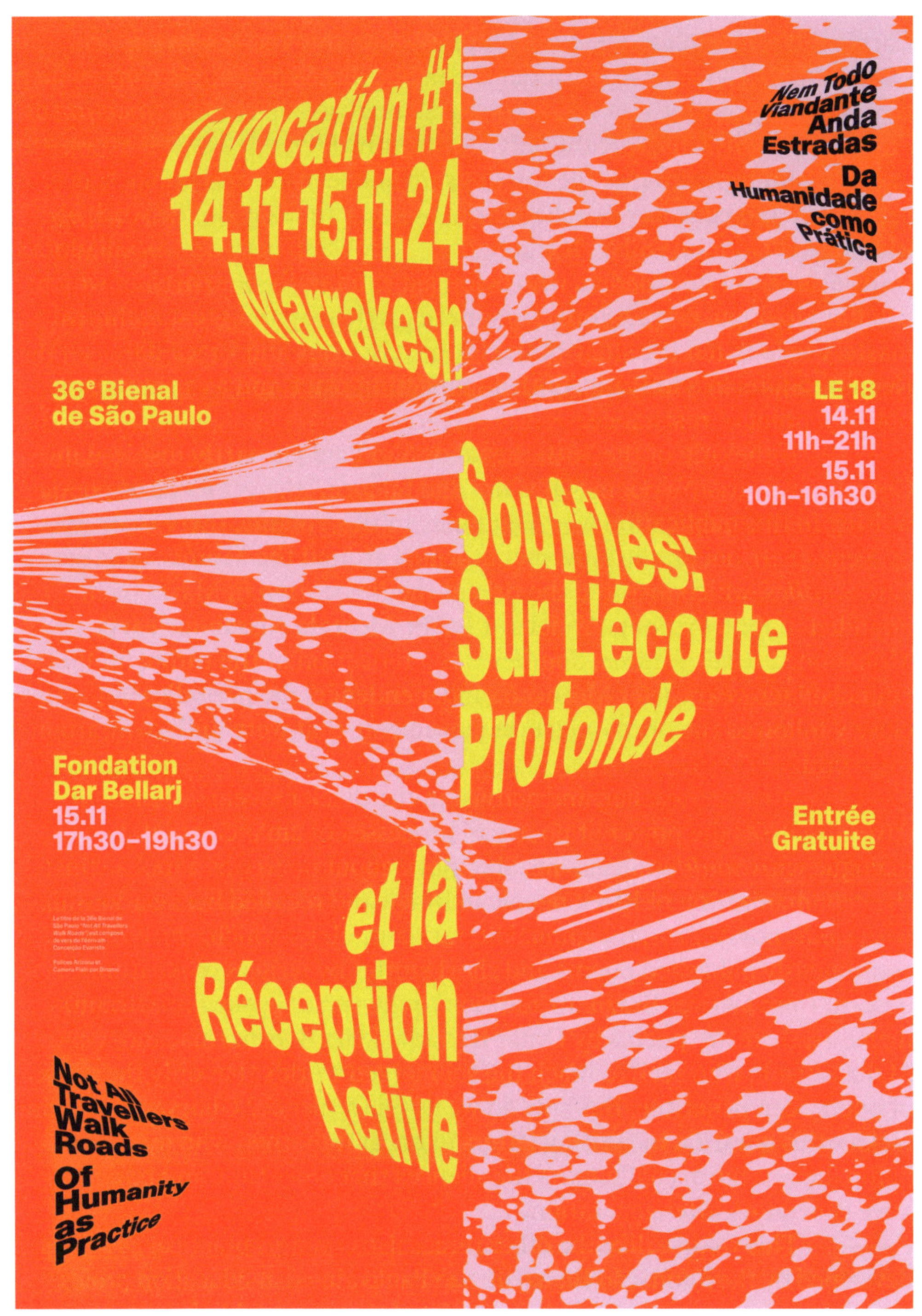

Poster for *Invocation #1*, Nov 14-15, 2024
© Studio Yukiko / Fundação Bienal de São Paulo

Carnival *blocos* such as Olodum, Filhos de Gandhy, and his own *bloco*, Cortejo Afro. Here, we learn about the public dimension of his work, which writes history on cloth for those who can't read, establishing a *"meeting of illiterates,"* in his words, at the Salvador Carnival.

And speaking of the relationship between art and public space, researcher and educator Mirella Maria presents an essay on the work of Maria Auxiliadora da Silva. It traces the relationship between Auxiliadora's transmissions of knowledge, who belonged to a family of artists, in which listening to popular traditions, personal experiences and great technical mastery help to tell the story of the Embu das Artes and Praça da República fairs in São Paulo, both as a meeting place and as a significant political point of resistance.

If the title of the 36th Bienal de São Paulo is partly inspired by Conceição Evaristo's poem "Of Calm and Silence," the presence of poetic writing in this publication was inevitable. In this volume, there is an essay by Kenza Sefrioui on the movement formed around the Moroccan magazine *Souffles*, which inspired the title of the *Invocation* in Marrakech. Founded in 1966 by poets Abdellatif Laâbi, Mostafa Nissabouri, and Mohammed Khaïr-Eddine, *Souffles* was a reflection of the turbulent 1960s. Launched ten years after Morocco's independence, the periodical closely followed the decolonization movements that were underway around the world.

A writer, teacher, and activist in the Black movement, Miriam Alves discusses the power of poetry in processes of emancipation, in dialogue with *Souffles* magazine. She spoke about poetry as a tool against the dehumanization of Black people in Brazil and recalled her relationship with *Cadernos Negros*, the annual literary anthology which, since 1978, has continuously published poems and short stories by writers of African descent from all over Brazil. In addition to the verses evoked in Miriam's memoirs, there are poems by Omar Berrada, Leila Bencharnia, and Maha Elmadi, who seek to reach the submerged worlds that only the silence of poetry can penetrate. But how do we listen to silence? Ghassan El Hakim tackles this question by writing letters to his grandfather, who died long before he was born, challenging the silences that cross time and remain alive generation after generation.

This volume, like the other three, also contains practical activities developed by the Fundação Bienal de São Paulo aimed at education professionals from various contexts, which seek to bring the world of contemporary art closer to formal and non-formal education.

The invitation to enter this book-*roda* also comes from verses by Conceição Evaristo, in her poem "The Wheel of the Not Absent":[2]

So I trace our spinning wheel
in which those of yesterday, those of today,
and those of tomorrow recognize each other
in each other's pieces.
Whole.

1   Gnawa is a traditional musical genre, predominantly practiced in Morocco, but also present in Algeria, Egypt, and Tunisia, which combines spiritual rhythms and chants, usually related to healing rituals and celebrations called *Lilas*. Its earliest records date back to the 16th century and today it carries influences from different musical genres, such as reggae, blues, hip-hop, and jazz, which was also influenced by the sound style of Gnawa music between the 1960s and 1970s. In 2019, Gnawa was recognized as an intangible heritage of humanity by UNESCO. This recognition highlights the importance of this musical genre as an essential element of Morocco's cultural heritage.

2   Conceição Evaristo, *Poemas da recordação e outros movimentos*. Rio de Janeiro: Malê, 2017, p.12.

How to Ventilate in an Airtight World

Bonaventure Soh Bejeng Ndikung

Reproduction of the
opening speech given on
November 14, 2024.

For this first *Invocation* in Marrakech, with the title
Souffles: On Deep Listening and Active Reception for the
36th edition of the Bienal de São Paulo, scheduled to take
place in São Paulo, Brazil, from September 2025 to
January 2026, I will convoke the spirit of the legendary
Indonesian poet Raden Mas Willibrordus Surendra Broto,
also known as Rendra.

      In 1960, Rendra wrote a poem which one
can read as the anthem of the 20th and 21st centuries,
with the captivating title "Sebuah Dunia Yang Marah"
[An Angry World].

      I would like to read out loud the poem, which was
an epitome of his time and is of our contemporary too,
while we listen to a song titled "You Ain't Gonna Know Me
'Cos You Think You Know Me," composed by another
legendary artist that I will like to convoke to be with us
for this *Invocation*, The Brotherhood of Breath's Mongezi
Feza. We will listen to a rendition by Feza's co-band
member Louis Moholo.[1]

Sebuah Dunia Yang Marah [An Angry World]

After two world wars
the chatter of guns and munitions in the air,
how does the world look now?
After so many speeches and conferences
the establishment of fine institutions
merely to quarrel
through a thousand slogans
and stab each other in the back,
how does the world breathe now?

Here in this part of the Earth
there are wounded faces
in the dark night of the spirit.
We do not need a map
to show where our people are.

This is an angry world.
Full of bright vicious eyes,
cruel hopeless faces,
and trembling hands
grasping at empty life.
In which
homes, men and rubbish
are all one.
Full of impotent bitterness.

World wars and rebellion
did not change our weary earth.
Murder after murder
hatred after hatred
gave birth to nothing
but sin, doubt,
and disbelief.

Gave birth to nothing
except the sacrifice of the powerless.
The continually questioning faces!
Driven into a world
of confusion and lies
they are always alone.
They grow from sin. They give birth to sin.

Our world is always wounded.
The poor walk with their hunger.
They are like thin dead sticks.
They regret their birth
but refuse to die.
They are sterile. They produce nothing.
They cling to the earth –
for that is their mother.
The others are their enemies.

In our tattered world
the poor beat out their bloody lives
suffering sin
unconsciously. Unwillingly.
God stands amongst them
He is wounded with them.
And the world rejects Him.
God cries with them.
But they do not hear Him.
God is sad and suffering
buffeted by angry feet.
Buffeted by bitterness
And restless fear.

Father!
Avoiding death
is their main problem
not welfare or sin.
How can they understand the voice of heaven
if they have never heard the voice of life?

31

Father!
While the world understands only guns and
deceit
stretch out Your loving hands
Your loving wounded heart.
Your wounds! Father, Your wounds!
Only through wounds
Can the world understand love.
God cries and understands.
God continually cries and understands.
He is always stabbed. Always betrayed.

Raden Mas Willibrordus Surendra Broto; W.S. Rendra, 1960[2]

Take 1

In this poignant and profound poem written more than 64 years ago, Rendra laments in utter awe the inscrutable state of the world today. The term "today" in its relativity and endless elasticity is that day, that week, that month, that moment in 1960 when the poem was written, and that point in time today, when you notice that the today of 1960 could easily step in as a surrogate for the today of now and vice versa. In this seminal poem, Rendra points at the hypocrisy and senselessness of speeches, conferences, institutions that offer lip service while the world crumbles under greed, betrayal, megalomania, kleptocracy, war, state supported terrorisms, genocides, environmental catastrophes and most viciously the violences of inactivity, passivity, and the deafening loudness of silences and silencing. He writes of despair, viciousness and empty lives. Of impotent bitterness. On forlornness on the face of the earth inhabited by hopelessness, hate, murder. Of a world haunted by lies, confusion and, for lack of a better term, sin. And at some point he breaks down, breaks it down and asks in a state of desolation – "how does the world breathe now?"

That this question forces us to reminisce on all the thousands and millions of humans whose breaths have been robbed from them in Cameroon, Congo, Mexico, Palestine, Rohingya, Sudan, Syria, Yemen, even our brothers and sisters unfair from here in Marrakech whose names we are not allowed to pronounce and all the citizens around the world that might or might not have screamed "I can't breathe" is neither a matter of haphazardry, nor a footnote in a narrative. Rather, Rendra's poem resonates with us so consequently today because it mirrors a humanity in a world struggling under the burden of misused power, of whiteness, of patriarchy, of misogyny, of racism, of coloniality and of theo-despotism. It is a poem that resounds what the Haitian poet Frankétienne calls the "Chaophonies of the world." A world stripped of its humanity. A world in which animals have come to have more decency and dignity than humans. A world, which as James Baldwin once put it: "is held together by the love and passion of a very few people." How does such a world actually breathe?

So, "how does the world breathe now," when, according to Vision of Humanity,[3] in just the first four months of 2024, 47,000 people lost their lives in conflicts worldwide, and if that continued in the same rate, 2024 would be the year with the highest number of conflict deaths since the Rwandan genocide in 1994. "How does the world breathe now," when the global economic impact of violence in 2023 was $19.1 trillion or $2,380 per person? "How does the world breathe now," when according to the Global Peace Index there are currently 56 conflicts around the world, the most since World War II (1939-1945), with 92 countries involved in conflicts outside their own borders, which is the most since the GPI's inception? "How does the world breathe now," in a world in which, according to recent UNHCR figures, 130.8 million humans have been forcibly displaced and are stateless?[4]

"How does the world breathe now," in an age when demagogues and protofascists around the world win democratic elections by preaching sermons about building walls between countries to keep out certain groups of people they consider rapists or not worthy of being human enough? "How does the world breathe now," in a time when despotic and theocratic leaders wage wars on neighboring peoples in some of the most dehumanizing contexts of warfare in which the lives of children, women, journalists, medical personal and aid workers are worth as much as nothing? "How does the world breathe now," when people all over the world are persecuted for their sexual orientations, the color of their skin, their religion or non-faith? "How does the world breathe now" in an era in which the prison system is an economic model, children are baits, citizens are pawns in geopolitical chess games, and humans are just commodities in a neoliberal economic establishment?

How does the world breathe now?

33

How could the world even breathe when in a bid to fulfil our long-ings for wealth, energy and comfort we destroy its veins and arteries; reap it of its resources; dehumanize other humans and commodify all that comes our way? How could it even think of breathing if the weakest in its ranks can barely feed themselves, but we can afford to vote for millionaires who want to send people on the moon for vacation...

As Gil Scott-Heron put it:

A rat done bit my sister Nell
With Whitey on the moon
Her face and arms began to swell
And Whitey's on the moon

I can't pay no doctor bills
But Whitey's on the moon
Ten years from now I'll be paying still
While Whitey's on the moon[5]

In this *Invocation* on "deep listening and active reception" may we bear witness, become catalysts and containers of sensibilities, possibili-ties, spirits and cognizances of causes that touch the nerves of our times. May we learn how to, or strive towards, a conjugation of humanity by acknowledging that we are not islands. That our humanity is only possible if we recognize and respect the humanity of others, and that we exist because others exist – both the living and the non-living.

Take 2

In 1964, a group of young South African men – Louis Moholo, Chris McGregor, Dudu Pukwana, Mongezi Feza, Johnny Dyani, Nikele Moyake and Maxine McGregor – left South Africa via Mozambique to France, in a constellation known as The Blue Notes, for the Juan-les-Pins jazz festival. Some of them were barely adults (Johnny Dyani and Mongezi Feza were just 18!) and it was the year 11 ANC leaders, including Mandela, were sentenced to life imprisonment, so the only chance they saw as a possibility to continue breathing was to go into exile.

"The Brotherhood of Breath" was born from Blue Notes, which was itself the culmination of three groups: Chris McGregor's septet, the Jazz Giants with Dudu Pukwana and Nick Moyake, and the Jazz Ambassadors with Louis Moholo. Getting out of South Africa was

34

one thing, but making it in Europe was completely different. Thanks to Dollar Brand later known as Abdullah Ibrahim, they could find an initial way out. Via Zurich, they came to London at Ronnie Scott's Club, and later to Copenhagen Montmartre Club. It might sound like a hyperbole to say that with their entrance into Europe in the mid-1960s, they radically impacted European music at large and what one could call jazz in particular.

This bunch of young men who had to leave their country because they couldn't breathe in the excruciatingly tight and racist corset of Apartheid found a home in music while in exile.

But exile is a bottomless pit, a house without foundations, a tree without roots, a space in which one loses one's self, one's identity, and sometimes one's humanity. How does one breathe in a world that is itself in exile from itself and humanity that no longer understands what it means to be human?

How do we engage in re-articulating and re-conjugating humanity in opposition to a violent notion of humanity forced upon us? That seems to me to might have also been the thoughts of the young South African jazz trumpeter and flautist Mongezi Feza, who died at just 30 in 1975, when he was composing the incredible piece about uncertainties "You Ain't Gonna Know Me ('Cos You Think You Know Me)."

1   The song can be found on YouTube at: www.youtube.com/watch?v=CJIP7nX_qtY. Accessed in: 2024.

2   Translated by Harry Aveling; courtesy of Lontar Foundation.

3   See: www.visionofhumanity.org/highest-number-of-countries-engaged-in-conflict-since-world-war-ii. Accessed in: 2024.

4   See: reporting.unhcr.org. Accessed in: 2024.

5   "Whitey on the Moon" is a spoken word poem by Gil Scott-Heron, released in his debut album *Small Talk at 125th and Lenox*, 1970.

The Sacredness of a Moment

Alya Sebti

*Ecoute plus souvent
Les Choses que les Êtres
La Voix du Feu s'entend,
Entends la Voix de l'Eau.
Ecoute dans le Vent
Le Buisson en sanglots,
C'est le Souffle des Ancêtres.*

[Listen more often
To the Things than to Beings
The Voice of Fire is heard,
Hear the Voice of Water.
Listen in the Wind
To the Bush in sobs,
It is the Breath of the Ancestors.]

37 "Souffles," Birago Diop

How does it feel when every cell of the body listens deeply?
What happens when bodies collectively remember; when
         rhythm, breaths, and silences fill the interstices
         of forgotten words?

These were some of the questions that guided our gathering in Marrakech, Morocco, under the title *Souffles: On Deep Listening and Active Reception.* If humanity can be a practice, a verb, let's remember the practice of deep listening, which, I claim, has its ancestral roots in Marrakech: the Gnawa culture, the tradition of Halqa[1] on Jemaa el-Fna square, and Sufi rituals and its poetry. During these days, we found ourselves immersed in a profound process of listening, in which each sound, gesture, and silence became a carrier of meaning and memory.

What memories do we evoke when we receive the rhythm of the musical instrument guembri, the presence of the Gnawa master Abdellah El Gourd and his charged silences, the tremors of Ghassan El Hakim – a healer on the cusp of being healed – reading his letters to the grandfather he never met, the deep frequencies of Leila Bencharnia's sound installation, the screams of Abdellatif Laâbi's poems read by Kenza Sefrioui, or the looped rhythms of bees called by Simnikiwe Buhlungu? To listen is to remember.

As we confront our childhood mythologies and their mixture of excitement and fear, how do we respond to Laila Hida's performative reading on the fiction and representation of the origins, accompanied by Mourad Belouadi's musical composition, or to the conversation imagined by Fatima-Zahra Lakrissa?

What happens when we allow our bodies to be carried by the unified chanting of a Hadra Sufi ritual sung by mothers, a healing through trance that crosses geographies?

These are not mere memories. They are echoes that transcend time and space, resonating in ways that dig deep into the layers of forgotten ancestral maps. They are moments of listening that connect us to histories older than our imaginations. These resonances carry the potential of futures yet to come.

At Dar Bellarj, during the final gathering of our two-day program, there was a moment in which the energy of these *Invocations* became palpable. The same group that had convened for the listening sessions, discussions, poetry readings, performances, meals, tears, and laughters was now in the courtyard of the Dar, under a full moon. The smell of oud filled the air. And the chanting began.

Led by Lalla Khala, singing master who had been training for years the mothers of Les Mamans Douées,[2] the rhythmic chants grew in intensity. At a certain point, one of the women from the collective felt called to stand up and started to dance. Slowly at first, then with increasing confidence, she fell into a trance. As the chanting crescendoed, the woman moved freely, carried by the rhythm and voices of the group. She knew she was not alone. She knew that she could trust the collective, and that their togetherness had the power to guide her on a journey of healing. She knew that she would be supported throughout.

The energy suddenly shifted as a single voice rose in the middle of the chant. Other voices joined, and the collective ended the moment by singing a song that carried both fierce joy and hope. This was the second time such an invocation had occurred during our time together. The first instance had been the previous evening, when Maalem El Gourd blessed us with his presence. That night I could hardly articulate the moment's meaning; I was too overwhelmed by the energy and the tears that flowed as I felt the power of a collective embrace. The second night, however, I could find words for what had transpired:

> This is to recognize the sacredness of a moment and to share it.
> Because there was trust.
> Because there was hope.
> Because there was joy.

What happened in that moment was not just a ritual or a performance, but the emergence of a space of vulnerability, communion, recognition and generosity. Here, the Hadra ritual was carried out by mothers whose joined voices wove a tapestry of trust and energy that could hold and heal. The act of falling into trance – of surrendering to the rhythm, spirit and collective energy – was an act of faith in the collective, in the shared power of the group to heal, support, and carry everyone through the journey.

This is what I mean by active reception: letting the body listen, letting it fall knowing that it will be carried. It is a profound act of surrender to something greater than the self. It is the act of trust, love, and opening, of making the body sentient and entering into a communion with the collective.

In reflecting on this experience, I find myself thinking about one of the Bienal's central concept figures, *Fragment II*, in which Leo Asemota asks, "When you look in the mirror, who do you see?"

I would like to slightly modify this question: who do you listen to?

At Dar Bellarj, thc chanting invoked not only the voices of those present, but also the spirits and ancestors that came before us and those yet to come. This is vertical connectedness – the alignment with our genealogies and lineages, a web of existence that stretches across time and space. The also-present horizontal connectedness is the sense of being one with the collective in a communal space of listening and trust. At this moment at Dar Bellarj, our bodies fell into rhythm with one another, connected by a common energy.

The chanting was a calling forth to the spirits – the ones who came before us – and a welcoming of those who would follow. The mothers were channeling those energies, offering us a way to feel held and connected across time.

In that instant, I was reminded of the words of poet René Depestre – another figure of the Bienal's concept:

> *Ma joie est de savoir que tu es moi et que moi je suis*
> *fortement toi.*[3]
> [My joy is to know that you are me and that I am deeply you.]

As we invoked and received the evening's energies, we were reminded of the power of listening – not just with our ears, but also with our bodies. We were carried and provided with the energy to go on; we were imparted with the blessing to channel the voices that accompanied us that night. Voices of ancestors, spirits, mothers, and one another.

May we carry these voices as we embark on our shared journey toward the Bienal de São Paulo and beyond. May there be trust, may there be hope, may there be joy.

1   Halqa: at the intersection between storytelling and agora.
2   The group was created in 2008 on the initiative of Maha Elmadi, Director of the Fondation Dar Bellarj. The idea of the group emerged to fight prejudices that reduce women to the roles of mothers or wives. The initiative also drew inspiration from Fatima Mernissi's Caravanes civiques, a network of Moroccan artists, intellectuals and activists fighting for the education of rural Moroccan women. According to the Mamans Douées, the "Mother" is a pivotal point in transmitting values. As the guardian of the collective memory, she bridges the gap between generations and welds the "social" family together. For the past ten years, their actions developed at Dar Bellarj through creative workshops, collaborative projects with artists, Sufi songs, theater, poetry, and handicraft.
3   René Depestre, *En état de poésie (Petite sirène)*, Les éditeurs français réunis, Éd. numérique, 2012, p.28.

Apuleius *Souffles,* Fifty Years On...

Kenza Sefrioui

In March 1966, the first issue of *Souffles* was published in Rabat. Hailed as "dynamite," the magazine changed the direction of the literary, artistic, and political world in Morocco and beyond. And it continues to challenge us.

A brilliant impulse. This is the image that comes to mind when thinking about the history of *Souffles*. In 1966, a group of mainly French-speaking poets, including Abdellatif Laâbi, Mostafa Nissabouri, and Mohammed Khaïr-Eddine, created a quarterly magazine to publish their innovative work. In January 1972, the magazine's main representatives were arrested, tortured, tried in collective trials in 1973 and 1977, and sentenced to long prison terms for attacking state security. Over the course of seven years, this initially poetic and artistic project developed and fulfilled its subversive potential, becoming more openly political and a tribune of the nascent Moroccan Marxist-Leninist movement. Even with the evolution between the first issues and those whose tone was one of radical protest, especially in its Arabic version *Anfas*, and even with the renewal of the team during the upheaval of 1969, *Souffles* remained coherent and faithful to its principles. Always a tribune of opposition to the project of the authoritarian and traditionalist power of the time, it formulated its progressive and modernist counter-project in a way that proposed a dynamic of hope. The hope of transforming man, of transforming the world. First, by introducing modern values into society through art and culture, in order to reform it profoundly; then through the revolution that the activists of organizations such as the *Ila al-Amam* Party and *23 Mars* dreamed of. Looking at *Souffles* today, one is struck by the strength with which its authors used culture as an engine for questioning and challenging, scrutinizing the foundations of politics and orienting it towards humanism and modernity.

Culture, A Driving Force

Souffles is a mirror of the effervescent 1960s. Launched ten years after Morocco's independence, it closely followed the decolonization movements that were still underway around the world. Palestine and Vietnam are emblems of the rejection of any form of imperialism, be it neo-colonialism or Zionism. *Souffles* dreamed of what it saw in Che Guevara, in the Chinese Cultural Revolution, and in May 1968, and was swept by these winds of freedom and desire for openness. It echoed the anger of a youth traumatized both by the repression in Morocco of any desire to protest (from the crushing of the student demonstrations in March 1965 to the assassination of Mehdi Ben Barka) and by the

43

defeat of June 1967 – a youth that was radicalized, that rejected bourgeois culture, and saw a way out in the revolutionary path proposed by Marxism-Leninism. It is true that the dogmatic tone that its pages took on in the last editions was criticized, but *Souffles*, with a manifesto-like rhetoric and an almost messianic tone, conveyed a mobilizing discourse that led this politicized generation, eager for debate, to dream and contributed greatly to its politicization. It was in this latter formula that its circulation grew from 1,000 to 5,000 copies, and many of these young activists went on to become the soul of civil society, working in the fields of human rights and culture. With the exception of the errors in their assessment of the political situation, their analyses are still relevant today: the authors clearly perceived the vices of underdevelopment in terms of misery, illiteracy, dependence on foreign powers, and the blockage of economic and political initiative. They understood the reinvention of traditions to support authoritarian power, they were concerned about disastrous educational policies and the absence of cultural policies…

44

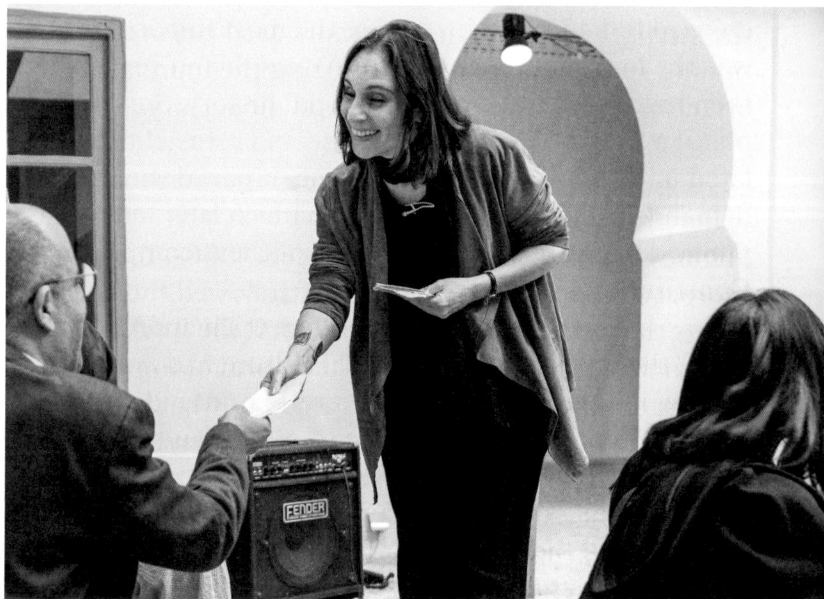

Decolonization and Opening

Souffles set out to complete Morocco's independence by decolonizing its culture. After the trauma of colonial rule, the aim was to restore its creative dignity. In "Le gâchis" [The Waste], an essential article published in the special issue dedicated to the visual arts (*Souffles*, No. 7-8), Abdellatif Laâbi makes a remarkable analysis of colonial science: he points out that this mass of documentation, intended to support the enterprise of domination, constituted an inventory of a heritage threatened by the profound transformations of society during the 20th century, but that its analysis needs to be completely revised. However, *Souffles* did not idealize the pre-colonial period: it championed creativity and was interested in what was modern. This resulted in its firm condemnation of any form of folklorization of culture that produced stereotypes ready to be consumed by tourists. Writers and artists then re-read popular culture, finding in the vitality of oral tradition or in the abstract power of traditional arts elements that anchored their contemporary concerns in heritage. In the same way, the magazine rehabilitated Driss Chraïbi, disgraced since the scandal caused by the publication of *Passé Simple* in 1954, in the midst of the struggles for independence. Tradition had indeed to be stripped of its archaisms – which ran counter to the official project, which at the time was based precisely on the revaluation of these archaisms in order to re-traditionalize society. *Souffles* sought to contribute to the creation of a modern popular culture, addressing an educated and conscious audience who enjoyed full citizenship. One of the most important aspects of its project was the implicit recognition of Amazigh and Jewish heritage, which was then hidden from Morocco's official history. *Souffles* insisted on the plural aspect of Moroccan culture and refused to allow it to be assimilated into Arabism and Islam alone. It paved the way for important demands from civil society, which much later led to the opening of public debate and the recognition of these components in the 2011 Constitution.

The magazine also took an open approach to identity. For them, the revaluation of national culture had nothing to do with narrow-minded culturalism or a retreat into identity. *Souffles* dreams of a culture that is open, attentive to others, and based on solidarity. The wealth of subscriptions from Algeria, Tunisia, Mozambique, Haiti, Argentina, etc. that it attracted demonstrates its openness to the world and the strength of its projection in relation to the causes and values it shares. By establishing itself as an important cultural

45

center in Morocco, it also highlighted the balance of power and the fact that Western culture is often considered to be universal.

A Radiant Pole

But if *Souffles* remains a key reference, it is undoubtedly first and foremost because of the strength of the cultural and intellectual movement that crystallized around it. It was a veritable writing laboratory, which helped to give the prose and free verse poems of Morocco and the Maghreb their due. Subjugated by the poetic power of Aimé Césaire, Frantz Fanon, and Kateb Yacine, these writers advocated writing that was a *seismic* organic experience capable of releasing an oppressed and stifled authenticity, of breaking with the wise lament or the *cahiers de doléances* that they saw in the works of the previous generation. We always read, with renewed pleasure, the texts of Abdellatif Laâbi, Mostafa Nissabouri, Mohammed Khaïr-Eddine, Mohamed Loakira, Ahmed Bouanani, Tahar Ben Jelloun, Mohammed Berrada, Mohammed Zafzaf, Driss El Khouri, to name but a few... On a literary level, there hasn't been a collective moment of equal intensity since.

 Souffles' strength also comes from its transdisciplinary experience, with its openness to cinema, theater, the visual arts, dance, etc., with the formidable complicity of artists from all disciplines. This has allowed a transversal reflection on common problems: the elitism of cultural circuits (art galleries, film clubs), how to reach different audiences, the role of foreign cultural institutes and the risks of acculturation, the lack of vision of a sustainable cultural policy, art in the street, etc. Its proposals, in particular the exhibition on the Jemaa el-Fna square in Marrakech in 1969, or the creation, following the magazine, of the Atlantes editions, made history.

 As a tribune, *Souffles* was known for its liveliness, its freedom of tone and its humor. It remains an ideal of freedom of expression and, if there is no longer a cultural magazine of this magnitude today, it was a model for the young independent press that briefly existed in Morocco at the turn of the millennium, and whose absence is now glaring. Finally, *Souffles* contributed greatly to the establishment of a new left-wing culture. Civil society, most of whose militants are former students of this adventure, remains attached to the values of progress, democracy, freedom, respect, humanism, human rights, social justice... And it did so with admirable courage, given that many of its authors, Abraham Serfaty, Abdellatif Laâbi, Abdelhamid Amine, Jamal Bellakhdar and so many young activists, endured severe repression (torture, long years in prison or exile) because of their commitment. What would we be today if this experience had not been abruptly interrupted? Interrupted, but not broken...

47

On Graphos and Ofó

Miriam Alves

Text developed from a
conversation between the
Fundação Bienal team and the writer on
November 19, 2024.

I always say that I started writing almost the way all children and teenagers do, by putting a poem down on paper, keeping a diary. I had a collection of little notebooks, between the ages of fifteen and twenty, any happiness, any annoyance, I would write it down, and I also invented a lot.

I think these are the basics. Then you understand that this is writing, that this is creation, that you don't necessarily have to write from a visible reality, you can imagine and write, but it took a long time before I reached the maturity of this thought. I stopped writing prose when I was fifteen, more or less, because of my technique of putting things on paper that didn't happen.

And so it went, notebooks and notebooks, late nights filling up paper and so on. Then there comes a time when you start writing and want to show it to people. At that point I was already studying social sciences. Then I would show them, everyone would get together on Fridays to play the guitar, have something to eat. It was our Friday night of staying out late in the bars near the college. And I was always reading my poems, you know?

"My flesh burned in the pan and all that," things like that. "My soul suffered in the hold of some ship, I scrape the white clay off with garlic straw..." and so on. It was a bit light, that sort of thing. Puerile. It was all very puerile.

49 My poem, according to some, had a lot of skin. So it wasn't a poem, because it was too saggy. It had skin.

Then I said: "Okay." My friends said: "Look, forget this notebook business, we're taking you to a poetry book launch." It was in the city center, near Praça da República.

When I arrived, it was beautiful! There were over a hundred Black people reciting poems and playing... They would play the *atabaque*, take a break, one of them would go on to recite and then come back, hit the *atabaque*, another would go on to recite and I'll never forget the music they played:

> In this poem circle,
> I want to see who'll join.
> Poem circle, aêê. Poem
> circle.
> In this poem circle
> I want to see who'll join.[1]

[Miriam recites the poem]

> Even if they turn their
> backs
> To my words of fire
> I won't stop shouting
> I won't stop
> I won't stop shouting
>
> Gentlemen
> I was sent into the world
> To protest
> No tinsel lies
> Nothing will silence me[2]

This poem is miles long, two pages long. It's by Carlos Assumpção,[3] who I always quote. It's called "Protest." And it's a poem that's been widely recited in Black circles since 1954. He's still alive, the poet is still alive, ok?! And the poem was only published in the 1980s. Black writers are accompanied by this poem. Since the Frente Negra,[4] Quilombhoje,[5] the time of the soirees, the slams.

And then I said: "This is where I'm staying." There's skin here, it's mine. This is my skin. I stayed and wherever they went, I went. The Quilombhoje of the time were Oswaldo de Camargo,[6] Paulo Colina[7] and Abelardo Rodrigues.[8]

The following year, remember that little book I used to carry around with me and that nobody published? I collected my wages and made *Meus momentos de busca* [My Moments of Searching]. My first independent book was the first in a series of thirteen so far. I was doing the math, I've been writing for 42 years, 44 contributions to national and international anthologies, including *Cadernos Negros*, and thirteen individual books. Forty-two plus thirteen is 55 publications.

When I turned forty, it was a really good year, because I took part in a lot of events and traveled a lot. And for these 42 years of literature, the publisher Fósforo proposed and published *Poemas reunidos*. This book contains more than 300 poems that I've published.

Seventy-two years old, 42 years into my career, with 55 books published, I don't think I've done anything else in my life except write, but I've done other things too.

I've always seen myself as a writer, but that desire you have... And it stays hidden when someone asks you what you want to be when you grow up. Back in my day, we used to say teacher. If I said writer, I think everyone would laugh. Because literary writing, to this day, is placed in an inaccessible place where only a few have the key to the secret of writing. The muses of literature only choose a few so that they have the key to writing. That's the idea of an impenetrable place.

Look, I really like writing, you know? Because, over these 42 years, I've discovered some very important things about writing. If they were half asleep in me, they've been revealing themselves every year, with every book.

With every book, especially novels, that I write, I am someone else. I go there to reach places of my own that I might never reach if I didn't write. And so I reach the places of others too.

The Social Imaginary About Black People in Brazil

When you talk about a Black person's childhood, people already relate it to hunger, and not that I played games, that I played in the garden, that I played on swings and walked on stilts, you know? No, they'll immediately make a correlation with hunger, and that I'm a survivor of the social phenomena of a badly divided society.

Look, I've been talking about changing the imaginary, but literature is not going to do it alone. The writer isn't going to do it alone, but we Black writers are collectively pushing to change these narratives. The way academia, the university, looks at our writing, with Black academics, has changed. There's already been a small change, it's not a big deal because I really want it. But I'm not talking about it alone anymore.

Especially the historical part, the story of the birth of this nation. As far as I'm concerned, I remember the engravings by Debret and Rugendas, a Black man beating another Black man, or a Black man with a yoke around his neck and being dragged, and the caption: "Slave masters punished runaway and unruly slaves…"

At that point, Black children at school were bullied. [...] The school still shows Black people being beaten up, and the whites were the masters and had the right to do it.

Literature doesn't do everything, but it does a small part [...]. So, each with their own weapon, as I say. For me, poetry and writing have various biases. As Black writers, with diversity, we take one of these biases, and that's what makes it beautiful.

Cadernos Negros

Cadernos Negros was first published in 1978. I wasn't there in 1978. Everyone thinks I invented it, I have nothing to do with it, I arrived in the fifth year of *Cadernos Negros*, and it was a book this small [indicating with her hands] on newsprint.

Cadernos Negros emerged in 1978, with other social movements that were fomenting in Brazil, exactly at the time of the opening up and the end of the civil-military dictatorship.

At the same time, the Movimento Negro Unificado[9] was taking place, and within the Movimento Negro Unificado [...] the Movimento de Literatura Negra Brasileira emerged, which was in the same place, on rua Maria José

[Bixiga, in São Paulo]. And there were several Black intellectuals there at that time. In that space, which started as a theater with Thereza Santos.[10] But as other people came in, the theater thing was just a catalyst, other things started to be discussed, political prejudices, etc.

We would receive books from Black people who had been exiled, or self-exiled in Angola and other countries, that were being made there. Poems from the time of *Negritude*, the whole movement, and also the movement in the United States. And that influenced us. And in these discussions [...] there were different poets, different writers, I remember that some people decided: let's put a collection and a book together! And Assumpção's poem, which had never been published, was published.

According to Hugo,[11] the name *Cadernos Negros* was based on the example of Carolina Maria de Jesus, who wrote in notebooks. He appropriated the practice of writing in notebooks, hence *Cadernos Negros*. The idea was notebooks, where you put your ideas, the school notebooks, remember? The poetry I mentioned, the diary.

And then *Cadernos Negros* No. 5 came along. This group, which met every Friday at Bar Mutamba and so on, broke up, because it was already one of the oldest groups. Cuti was still making the notebooks. Remember when I said that I joined "Roda Poema, aê"? I arrived at that moment when it broke up. Esmeraldo[12] and I arrived, and the first thing we did was say: "Oh, Cuti, you doing *Cadernos Negros* alone isn't going to work, we want to do it together." So we divided up the roles.

And then there was the old Quilombhoje, the one that was arriving. There was a break, because those who were arriving were the youth of the time, 30-somethings, Cuti too, the others were older, especially Oswaldo, with all due respect. And there was a different way of looking at this work, and this literary work, this making notebooks and things like that, so much so that they made the *Axé* anthology, I was in *Axé literatura negra brasileira.*

Cadernos Negros also had to go to Black *bailes*. We would go to the Black *bailes*, take the microphone and perform poetry, sell books. And it grew, it grew in a very cool way, because every time we went to the *bailes*, we prepared a list of names and addresses to invite people to the launch, to be writers, to writers' meetings, where we could discuss our literature.

Apart from that, Quilombhoje met every Saturday, every Sunday, to discuss poems, [...] and we didn't just discuss, we wrote. When I think about it, we made our own academia, you know? Our academy of Black letters. And the white academic intelligentsia started to join in. But we had our own codes, our own rules. *Cadernos Negros* was Black-only. Because we didn't want to be the object of study. We wanted to be the subject of our speech, of our writing. And things grew. In this sense, we broke some paradigms: Black people don't read. Black people don't write. Black people don't buy books. So I agree that Black people don't read. They don't read anything that doesn't interest them!

Many unpublished writers also ended up in *Cadernos Negros*. A space grew, both the space in the book and the mental space. We were making a new geography. And we also made a new geography in the panorama of white Brazilian literature. Because you know when you're forced to talk about someone and you don't want to, but if someone is on your doorstep screaming and shouting, you have to talk about them, you know?

Orality and Writing

There is no antagonism between orality and writing, this antagonism was created. Why is that? Because our culture has an African matrix. Muslims, for example, had things written down in libraries and so on. In Africa, most cultures were oral. When we talk about oral culture, people think of people who have no culture. Orality was and is our culture. Where are the things from our roots, our cultures, passed on?

I have a text from when *Graphos abraçou Ofó* [Graphos embraced Ofó]. *Graphos* from writing and *Ofó* from the breath of the word, from Iansã, which the poet gives. When *Graphos* embraced *Ofó*, they went on a spree, and a piece of poetry came out of it. I feel like that. *Graphos* embracing *Ofó*, because in my work I use a lot of things I hear and have been told, from my mother, my grandmother, from the *terreiro*. Orality was a way of being informed, of knowing. Orality is wisdom. Many things that are reproduced now, even in writing, came from orality, which is wisdom.

Do you know what the issue with art is? The art of orality, painting, and sculpture of African origin? Because [African art] had no author. I don't sign underneath. This is Francisco's. No, this is from community X. All that wisdom led the artist to make that mask. Now, the mask that's in the Louvre belongs to the people. Understand? You're already putting things in places where they don't belong. Capitalism distorts things, because you have to be an individual. You have to be one.

53

1   A song sung at the Poem Circle, by an unknown author.

2   Carlos Assumpção, "Protesto," in *Não pararei de gritar: poemas reunidos*. São Paulo: Companhia das Letras, 2020.

3   Teacher, lawyer, poet and writer. Born in the city of Tietê (SP) in 1927, he lived in Franca, where he studied Literature and later Law. He collaborated on various magazines and publications by Black writers, including *Cadernos Negros*. *Protesto*, his first publication, was released in 1982. He is one of the most acclaimed writers in Brazilian poetry, as well as a dean.

4   The Frente Negra Brasileira (FNB) was created in October 1931 in the city of São Paulo. It was one of the first organizations in the 20th century to demand equal rights and participation for Black people in Brazilian society. Under the leadership of Arlindo Veiga dos Santos, José Correia Leite and others, the organization developed various political, cultural, and educational activities for its members. See ipeafro.org.br/acervo-digital/documentos/antecedentes-do-ten/frente-negra-brasileira.

5   A group founded in 1980 by Oswaldo de Camargo, Paulo Colina, Abelardo Rodrigues and others. The group's activities have varied over time, but they all consist of supporting and promoting the production, dissemination and research of Black literature and culture. Since its creation, the group has been responsible for the publication of *Cadernos Negros*.

6   Poet, writer, critic and historian of Brazilian literature. He was born in 1936 in the city of Bragança Paulista (SP). After a humanistic and erudite education in seminars in the inner state of São Paulo, he moved to the capital and began working for several newspapers, including *O Estado de S. Paulo* as a proofreader and *Jornal da Tarde* as an editor. Along with the Black movement, he was cultural director of the Associação Cultural do Negro and one of the main contributors to the Black press.

7   Poet, writer, playwright, translator, political and cultural activist. Paulo Eduardo de Oliveira or Paulo Colina (1950-1999), was born in Colina (SP), and was one of the founders of Quilombhoje. The publication of *AXÉ: antologia contemporânea de poesia negra brasileira* [AXÉ: Contemporary Anthology of Brazilian Black Poetry] in 1982 won the APCA (Associação Paulista de Críticos de Artes) award in the best poetry book category, making him a key figure of Brazilian Black literature.

8   Writer, poet, one of the founders of Quilombhoje. Born in Monte Azul Paulista (SP) in 1952, his work has been published in several volumes of *Cadernos Negros*.

9   The Movimento Negro Unificado (MNU), founded in June 1978, was one of the first organizations created to defend the Black population in Brazil. The milestone was the group's public demonstration on

the steps of the Theatro Municipal de São Paulo on July 7, 1987, in the midst of the military regime.

10   Philosopher, actor, playwright, carnival performer, she was active in the Communist Party and in the defense of African and Afro-Brazilian peoples. Born in Rio de Janeiro in 1930, she was a member of the Teatro Experimental do Negro and studied philosophy at the Faculdade Nacional de Filosofia, where she also joined the União Nacional dos Estudantes. In the 1960s, she went into exile in Mozambique, Guinea-Bissau and Angola, where she worked on educational and cultural projects and founded the first theater school in Angola. She moved to São Paulo after being arrested and persecuted in Rio de Janeiro, in 1969.

11   Hugo Ferreira, one of the founders of the group alongside Cuti.

12   Esmeraldo Ribeiro was born in São Paulo in 1958 and is still at the head of Quilombhoje. He was part of the movements against racism and collaborated in the construction of Afro-Brazilian literature.

Educational Activities

The activities in the educational publication for the 36th Bienal de São Paulo were developed with the aim of bringing the world of contemporary art closer to different pedagogical contexts. Prepared as scripts for holding creative laboratories, they are structured into three sessions that can be adapted and incorporated according to needs and possibilities.

In dialog with teachers of the São Paulo public school system[1] and Brazilian National Common Core Curriculum (BNCC) guidelines, the activities encourage the construction of integrated knowledge, the expression of ideas, feelings, and reflections on social and cultural issues. Inspired by the concept of *escrevivência*[2] and combined with the methodologies of the Museu da Pessoa,[3] the activities aim to promote an education that recognizes subjectivity and the plurality of experiences, understanding the participants as protagonists of the processes.

Poetry Circle

The activity aims to invite participants to relate to the contents of the educational publication, specifically the poems and the transcribed conversation with the writer Miriam Alves, as well as a poetry creation laboratory with reading exercises and experimentation with fanzines.

OBJECTIVES:

→ Research on *Cadernos Negros* – Quilombhoje Literatura
→ Telling and listening to stories
→ Creating poems and/or poetic texts
→ Developing individual, collective and collaborative creative processes

REQUIRED MATERIALS:

→ Sulfite paper or similar
→ Writing materials (graphite pencils, felt-tip pens)
→ Scissors and glue
→ Magazines and newspapers for cutting out
→ Computer, multimedia projector, and a loudspeaker

DEVELOPMENT:

The last lines of Conceição Evaristo's poem "Of Calm and Silence" say that "there are submerged worlds,/ that only the silence/ of poetry penetrates." In fact, with its silences – and its stirrings – poetry is able to penetrate human reality, to imagine other ways of living and of creating other worlds beyond the one we live in. It was with this awareness that the first volume of the *Cadernos Negros* series was published on November 19, 1978. Since then, there have been more than forty volumes, published annually, alternating between poems and short stories by Afro-descendant writers from all over Brazil.

Since the 1980s, *Cadernos Negros* has been published by Quilombhoje Literatura, a collective dedicated to the promotion of Black literature and the visibility of Afro-Brazilian writers. In addition to publishing, the collective organizes courses, seminars and debates on literature, among other activities. Here we highlight the poetry circle, an initiative that proposes a meeting between writers and the public, creating a space where the word, declaimed or sung, circulates among people who wish to express themselves poetically. Inspired by this action, this practice proposes a laboratory for the creation of poems, with reading exercises and experimentation with fanzines.

SESSION 1 – CADERNOS NEGROS – QUILOMBHOJE LITERATURA

The first workshop session begins with a discussion of the experience of the writer Miriam Alves, one of the leading figures in *Cadernos Negros*. We recommend that the class form a circle and read together the text of the conversation with the author that is included in this publication. The mediator can include texts and videos of interviews with other writers to encourage a conversation about poetic writing.

Once the reading is finished, have a chat about the material. If possible, write down impressions. Here are some suggested questions for the conversation: *How is the experience of writing told in these stories? How do you see the relationship between writing and identity?*

Research and select poems for the next session and ask the class to do the same.

SESSION 2 – POETRY CIRCLE

The second stage of the workshop involves a round of reading and listening to poems by different writers. At the beginning of the session, organize the poetry you have previously researched into a collection.

The poetry circle can be held as follows:

→ Plan the duration of the poetry circle, depending on the time available for the session
→ Introduce the proposal for the poetry circle: reading and listening to poems by different writers
→ Arrange the group in a circle and place the selected poems in the middle of the circle
→ One person at a time chooses a poem at random and recites it aloud to the group
→ The others write down words that grab their attention
→ A poem can be read more than once

We suggest that at the end of the poetry circle, the participants talk about the experience. Organize the class into small groups and encourage them to create poetic texts from their notes. Set aside for the next session.

SESSION 3 – POEM FANZINES

The first volume of *Cadernos Negros* was a small-format publication known as a pocket edition. For the third session, we propose the creation of fanzines – independent, handmade and inexpensive publications.

To develop the content of the fanzines, return to the groups from the previous session and continue creating poetic texts based on the notes taken during the poetry circle.

To make the fanzines, instruct the class as follows:

→ Use A4 sheets of sulfite paper and prepare the material as shown in the illustration
→ Using pens, colored pencils, or other possible tools, write on the prepared material the poems they created
→ Combine the poetic text production with illustrations/drawings, collages based on images from magazines/newspapers, or other graphic possibilities
→ If possible, bring in fanzines to inspire the class's creativity

Once production is complete, encourage participants to exchange fanzines and talk about the creative process.

SUGGESTIONS FOR FURTHER DEVELOPMENT:
Scan/photocopy the fanzines produced, print a number of copies and distribute them. It could be possible to hold a poetry circle with the fanzines created and encourage the practice of soirees based on them.

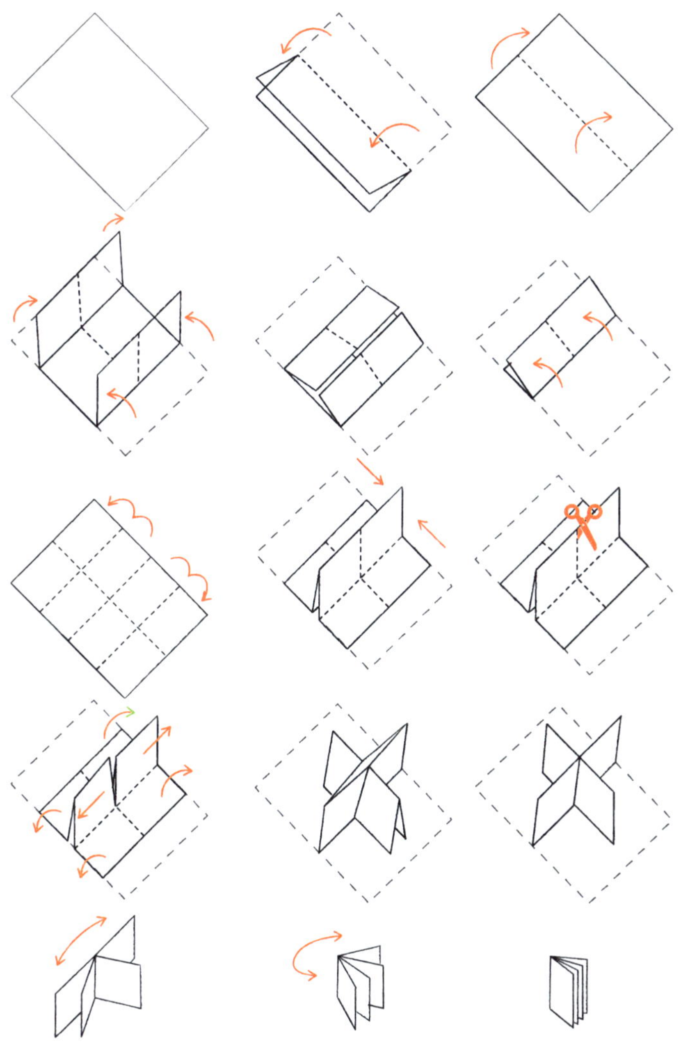

Story Circle

This practice aims to invite participants to create, tell, and listen to stories inspired by the work of the artist Maria Auxiliadora and their own experiences.

OBJECTIVES:

→ Research the work of the artist Maria Auxiliadora
→ Tell and listen to stories
→ Describe characteristics of the places where they live
→ Develop individual, collective and collaborative creative processes

REQUIRED MATERIALS:

→ Sulfite paper or similar
→ Writing materials (graphite pencils, felt-tip pens)
→ Computer, multimedia projector, and loudspeaker

DEVELOPMENT:

The proposal of the 36th Bienal de São Paulo is based on the idea of thinking of humanity as a verb, a living practice, in a world that requires a reimagining of relationships and using listening as a basis for coexistence. In this sense, when we talk about listening, we are not just referring to hearing, but to an attentive and generous attitude towards the people and environments that surround us.

63 The works of Maria Auxiliadora illustrate this perspective well, as they are vivid records of the painter's wanderings. Born into a family of artists who sold their work at the art fairs in Embu das Artes and Praça da República, in São Paulo, Auxiliadora learned to read and write as an adult, worked as a domestic servant, became a well-known painter, and died at the age of 39. In this exercise, people will be able to imagine, tell, and listen to stories inspired by the work of the artist and their personal experiences.

SESSION 1 – MARIA AUXILIADORA AND HER WANDERINGS

The first stage of this practice is a proposal to get to know the life and work of Maria Auxiliadora. Born in Campo Belo (MG) in 1935, Auxiliadora moved with her family to São Paulo when she was still a child. She grew up in the capital accompanying her parents who sold paintings and sculptures at the Praça da República market. It wasn't long before she and her siblings became interested in artistic creation. Unable to live exclusively from art, it was common for Auxiliadora and her family to have other jobs. The different environments in which the artist circulated were integrated into her poetics, revealing her discerning eye.

To get closer to the life and work of Maria Auxiliadora, we suggest arranging the group into a circle to listen to (or read) the *sound collage* that introduces the artist Maria Auxiliadora through dialogues (access via the QR Code). Still in a circle, we recommend that you start a conversation about the elements that appear in the audio (or text). Provide space for all participants to share their impressions. Here are some suggested conversation questions: *What places did Maria Auxiliadora pass through? Do you know any of them? Does this story resemble your own or that of someone you know? How do you imagine Maria Auxiliadora's paintings?*

At the end of the session, display the portrait of Maria Auxiliadora (accessible via the QR Code) and invite the class to research more about the artist. The essay by Mirella Maria about the artist, included in this publication, can be used for this purpose.

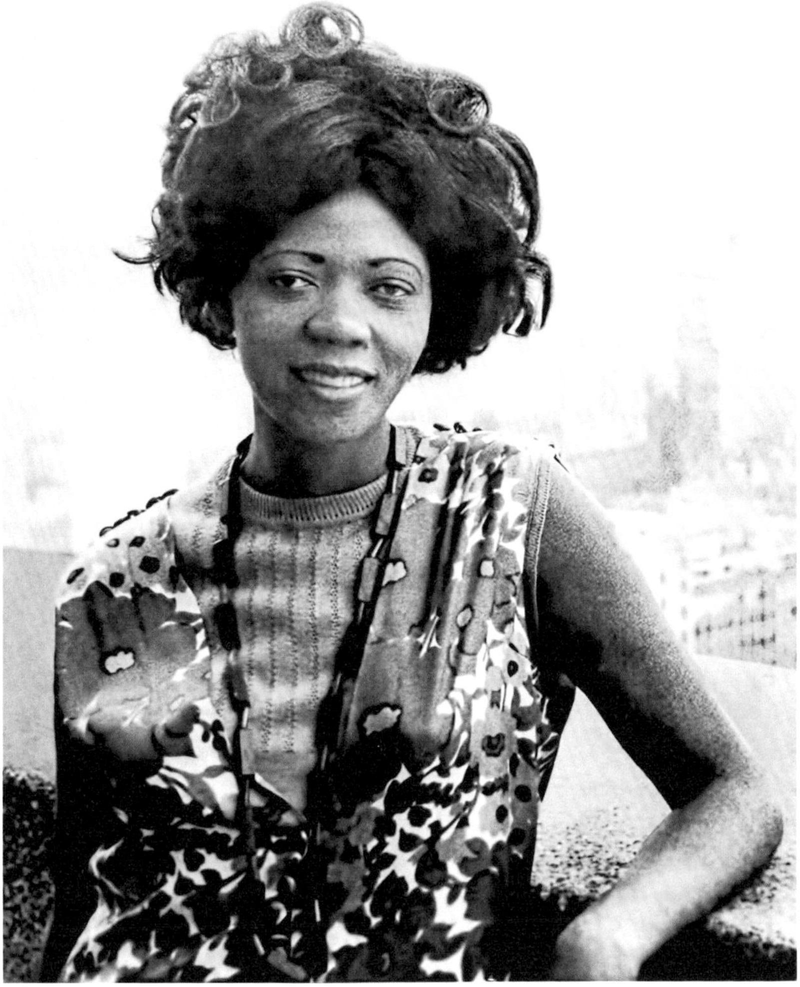

Maria Auxiliadora, undated
Photo: Emanuel von Lauenstein Massarani and
Patrick Goetelen
Courtesy: Pedro Ivo Silva and MASP

Scan the QR Code to access Maria Auxiliadora's
sound collage and other contents.

SESSION 2 – SPACES OF SOCIABILITY

Begin this stage with a round of sharing the possible research carried out by the class on Maria Auxiliadora. It's important to gather people's impressions and discoveries at this point. Next, show *Parque de diversões* [Amusement Park], from 1973. If possible, project the image of the work and read the description of the image to the class (accessible via the QR Code).

We suggest talking about the work using questions such as: *What is the environment depicted by the artist like? What scenes are taking place in the work?*

As discussion moves around the group, bring up aspects of the research you've done previously and point out questions about Maria Auxiliadora's life and work. For example, the fact that the artist painted not only amusement parks, but also squares, beaches, and streets full of life. For this reason, Auxiliadora became known as a painter who portrayed the daily lives of Black people from the countryside and the city, with an eye for work, but also for parties, carnivals, and entertainment in general.

After analyzing the picture, we suggest taking a moment for the group to look at their own reality, their memories, and their desires. To do this, we suggest questions such as: *Which places of entertainment do you and the people you know go to? What do you usually do there? What would you change, or what do these places lack, and you wish they had?*

Suggest that the class record their answers, especially the possibilities for action in the territories mentioned, and set them aside for the next session.

SESSION 3 – STORY CIRCLE: MARIA AUXILIADORA AND I...

The last stage of the activity is the story circle. This action is based on the image of the work *Parque de diversões* by Maria Auxiliadora and the notes from the previous session.

The story circle is an invitation for participants to imagine and share an encounter with Maria Auxiliadora in a setting that could be either the amusement park in the artist's painting or the leisure spaces mentioned in the previous session.

In order to do this, the person responsible for the mediation can make some choices, taking into account the time available for the action and the willingness of the participants:

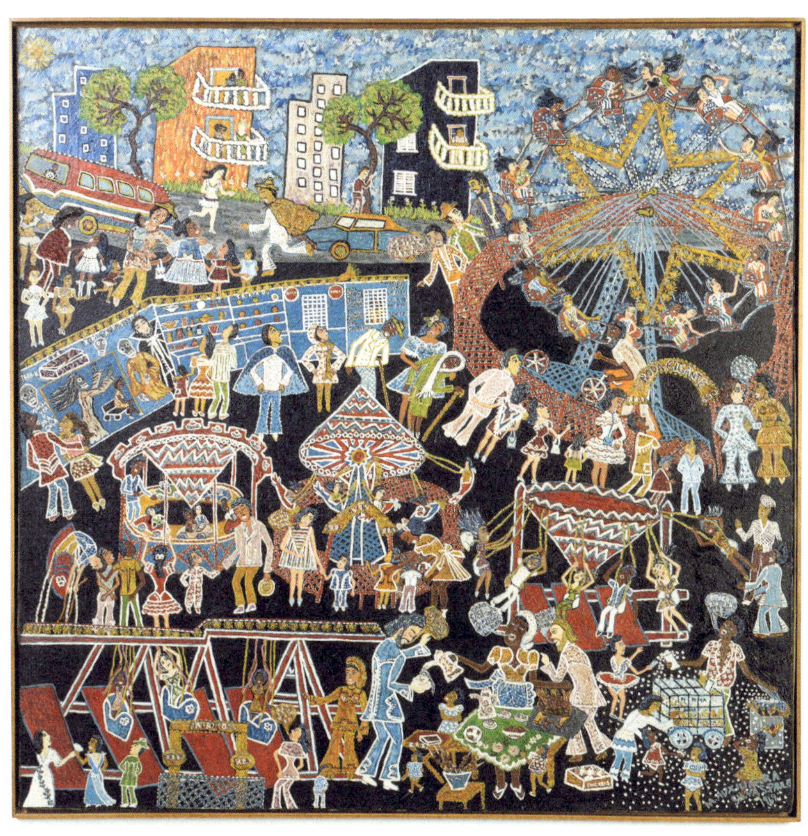

Parque de diversões [Amusement Park], 1973
Mixed media, 140 × 140 cm
Collection: Museu do Sol, Penápolis, SP
Photo: Maurício Froldi

67 Courtesy: Pedro Ivo Silva and MASP

- → Hold just one round in which each participant invents and shares a story with Maria Auxiliadora at the amusement park
- → Hold just one round in which each participant invents and shares a story with Maria Auxiliadora at the leisure spaces mentioned in the previous session
- → Or hold two rounds, one in which each participant invents and shares a story with Maria Auxiliadora at the leisure spaces mentioned in the previous session, and the other with a story with Maria Auxiliadora at the amusement park

The story circle can be carried out as follows:

- → Announce the proposal for the story circle and give people time to create their stories
- → Have the group form a circle
- → In the case of a story circle with the work *Parque de diversões*, provide a reproduction or project the image of the painting for the class
- → It is very important to agree on attention for the story circle. Listening to people's stories without interruptions is what will ensure that the story circle runs smoothly
- → Use words or phrases to mark the beginning and end of each story, such as: "When a person begins their story, they should say: "Maria Auxiliadora and I..." and when they finish, they should say: "Maria Auxiliadora and I..."
- → If possible, make an audio recording of the story circle

At the end of the activity, begin a conversation about what emerged from the story circle. The person responsible for mediating the meeting can encourage reflection on the activity. Some questions which may be useful in this process are: *How do the artist and the people in the group appear in these stories? What relationships were created between them? How do the environments known to the people in the group appear in the stories? How do they relate to Auxiliadora's work?*

Based on the stories created by the class, prepare scripts for the production of different types of content (music videos, documentaries, animations, etc.), theatrical presentations, multimedia and transmedia narratives, podcasts, commented playlists, etc.

This process can also be adapted to propose a dialog with territories, collaborating with the creation of affective cartographies of the places where they take place.

1 The Fundação Bienal would like to thank Bel Borges, Durval Mantovaninni, Gustavo Viana, Kaya Fernanda Vallim Braga Martins, Maria da Conceição Ferreira da Silva, Pamela Regina, and Rodrigo Pignatari for the rich exchanges that took place on October 26 and November 9, 2024.

2 The concept of *escrevivência*, developed by the writer and professor Conceição Evaristo, represents an intersection between the fictional narrative and everyday experience, especially of historically silenced bodies and voices, with a view to recovering forgotten narratives and building new identities. The word is a combination of "writing," "living" and "seeing oneself," reflecting an approach that goes beyond mere autobiography, as it seeks to incorporate the collective experience of the Black population and transform it into literature. See Conceição Evaristo, *Becos da memória*. Rio de Janeiro: Pallas, 2017, p.200.

3 Since 1992, the Museu da Pessoa has been dedicated to the development and dissemination of methodologies for the collection, preservation, and socialization of life stories. Learn more about the institution at museudapessoa.org.

From the Square to the Park, from the Park to Memories, from Memories to the Collective and Creative Paths of Maria Auxiliadora

Mirella Maria

Among Squares and Struggles

The theme of the 36th Bienal de São Paulo is *Not All Travellers Walk Roads – Of Humanity as Practice*, the first part of which is taken from the poem "On Calm and Silence" by Conceição Evaristo.[1] This powerful text invites us to reflect on the vital importance of pause and reflection in a world that constantly pressures us for movement and incessant production. Through this poem, Evaristo presents us with a kind of artistic manifesto that advocates for a creative process that respects the time needed for ideas to mature. From this perspective, we can better understand and appreciate the unique work of Maria Auxiliadora da Silva,[2] an artist who created her own path in the history of Brazilian art.

The Brazil of the 1970s, the period in which Maria Auxiliadora developed her work, was under military dictatorship. The "economic miracle"[3] touted by the regime masked profound social inequality, while growing urbanization rapidly transformed the landscapes of Brazil's major cities. In this context of social and urban transformation, São Paulo's Praça da República emerged as a vital territory of cultural resistance, especially for the Black population, who used the space to express themselves and sell their work.[4] It was in this context that Auxiliadora, at the age of 35, together with other creators, including artists from Embu das Artes[5] such as Solano Trindade, transformed the square into a significant artistic and political meeting place.[6] This period also marked the emergence of key organized Black movements, such as the Movimento Negro Unificado,[7] which began to openly question the supposed harmony between different racial groups due to miscegenation in the country, known as the myth of racial democracy.[8]

In the field of art, the 1970s were marked by intense debates about Brazilian art's identity. While official institutions privileged certain forms of expression, academic categorizations such as "popular," "naif" and "primitive" were often applied to artists such as Maria Auxiliadora.[9] As Renata Felinto points out in "A ideia de naif como estratégia decolonial," these classifications reflected a problematic hierarchization of the artistic system, which tended to marginalize creators without academic training, especially those of Black and peripheral origin. Felinto proposes a political re-reading of these works as transmitters of knowledge and technologies through generations via non-academic means.

This transmission of knowledge is evident in her biographical trajectory. Maria Auxiliadora da Silva was born in 1935 in Campo Belo, Minas Gerais, and raised in São Paulo from childhood. Her family history is deeply intertwined with the arts in their various manifestations, fed by the oral/visual memories that circulated in her family life. Her grandmother, Marcelina Carlota, was a samba dancer and dressmaker who brought musicality and handicraft techniques to the family environment. Her grandfather, José de Almeida, worked in wood carting, contributing another type of artisanal knowledge. Her brothers[10] were dedicated to painting, sculpture, and music, creating an environment of intense artistic production. Her mother, Maria Trindade de Almeida Silva, was a key figure in her artistic training, especially in teaching her embroidery techniques when she was just nine years old.

Between Times and Perspectives: Layered Narratives

Maria Auxiliadora's artistic work, nourished by her family's rich visual background, materializes significantly in *Parque de diversões* [Amusement Park] (1973). The work can be analyzed on three different and complementary levels:

In the foreground, located at the top of the canvas, we see the dynamic movement of a city in full swing: a colorful array of buildings with their windows and balconies looking out onto the street, cars driving along the roads, people walking on the sidewalks. This upper plane sets the urban scene and creates an important social context, showing how the city's routine is integrated with the leisure space present in this painting.

In the central plane, we find the work's beating heart: the amusement park itself. The artist captures the energy of this popular leisure space with an imposing Ferris wheel on the right, bumper cars on the left, and various other attractions. The colorful rides and clothing enrich the interaction between the space and the leisure objects and the people who use them and talk to each other, producing a rich view of exchange and coexistence.

At the bottom of the canvas, Maria Auxiliadora continues the visual description of the amusement park, where we see more toys to the left of the painting, a popcorn cart to the right, and in between, intimate scenes of people gathered for a kind of picnic. The frame of the work, though discreet, helps us to focus our gaze and attention on the details of the painting.

Materialities and Memories

Maria Auxiliadora's technical uniqueness, analyzed by Lélia Frota Coelho,[11] is revealed in her innovative combination of materials and procedures. On a base of oil paint built up in successive layers, the artist incorporates three-dimensional elements using plastic mass (polyester), creating reliefs that project the figures outwards from the canvas. Her originality extends to the use of unconventional materials – strands of natural hair, fabrics and lace – which dialogue directly with the memories and narratives explored in her work.

As Renata Felinto points out in "Maria Auxiliadora: o pisar sensível, existências do invisível e visualidades do indizível,"[12] her artistic language dialogues with both popular traditions and sophisticated visual representation techniques. Here I add that this political re-reading emphasizes the production of affective memories of the Black majority population in this work. It's a way for the artist to translate the narratives she had in her family, her personal experiences and those of other people as a way of perpetuating a visuality of the Black population with a degree of dignity and exaltation. We can thus delight in and perpetuate the memories of Maria Auxiliadora's *Parque de diversões*, its rides, the encounters and experiences portrayed there, and combine such visual power with our own memories, our parks, our moments of gathering and learning about the power of being with others and strengthening oneself against the denial of a basic right: to have fun, to exist in time and space.

From the Park to the Classroom: Educational Paths

Maria Auxiliadora's work offers rich educational possibilities that can be adapted to different contexts: classrooms, educational visits to museums, and workshops in cultural centers or educational institutions.[13] The initial approach to her work can be developed through detailed observation and open dialogue, where students are invited to share their impressions and memories evoked by the image through themes such as the maturation and production time of an artwork, encounters, experiences, and developments in public and collective leisure/entertainment spaces. This sensory approach is especially powerful in educational visits to museums, where direct contact with the work greatly enhances the experience.

Experimenting with different materials is another fundamental part of the educational task. Inspired by Maria Auxiliadora's characteristic mixed media technique, students can explore different creative possibilities by combining painting, collage, and textile materials.

In addition, the students' own plastic experiences from their cultural backgrounds can be part of this visual creation. The process of practical experimentation can develop into a visual documentation of contemporary leisure spaces, building bridges between Auxiliadora's work and contemporary reality.

The creation of collective visual narratives emerges as a proposal in which educators and students can develop works that represent their own experiences of leisure and coexistence. The social issues present in the work can be explored with discussions about the right to leisure and the use of public spaces, debates that are present both in the occupation by artists such as Maria Auxiliadora in the Praça da República on Sundays, and by contemporary collectives that make use of collective spaces to enjoy leisure, socializing, and listening.

The interdisciplinary possibilities expand when we connect the work with different areas of knowledge. The historical context of the 1970s in Brazil, urban transformations and the occupation of space, discussions about the right to leisure for the Black population and their powerful cultural manifestations in the city, as well as the production of mixed artistic techniques, can all be explored in an integrated way, enriching the educational experience.

Maria Auxiliadora: A Traveller on Her Own Path

Returning to the title of the 36th Bienal de São Paulo, Conceição Evaristo, through her poetry and especially in the verses contained in *Not all Travellers Walk Roads* broadens our perception in understanding how Maria Auxiliadora created her own path in Brazilian art. With a solid artistic foundation built in communion with her family, friends from Embu das Artes and Praça da República, she developed a unique technique that shows how it is possible to innovate from her artistic knowledge. Her work continues to inspire new generations of artists to seek their own forms of expression, valuing their stories and experiences.

As Renata Bittencourt points out in her article "Eu pinto crioulos,"[14] Auxiliadora was able to visually materialize the narrative of a Black woman through her own history, desires and insertion into the world. This perspective helps us understand how her work remains a historical and artistic document that invites us to reflect on issues that are still present in our society: the right to leisure, access to public spaces, and the dignified representation of the Black population.

74 Looking at *Parque de diversões* today, we are invited to reflect not only on the Brazil of the 1970s, the Praça da República and its exhibitions and artists' fair, but also on our own relationship with our time and space in terms of the presence of diverse bodies at leisure, occupying public spaces, circulating together in the city. The work challenges us to think about what spaces of joy and coexistence we build in our memories, in our cities, and how we can make them accessible and welcoming for and with everyone. Maria Auxiliadora's legacy remains alive and necessary, reminding us of the importance of pausing and remembering to create and maintain powerful places where the Black population is truly celebrated in its existence.

1   Conceição Evaristo, one of Brazil's most important contemporary writers, was born in Belo Horizonte in 1946. The creator of the concept of "escrevivência," her literary work is characterized by the intersection of race, class, and gender, with an emphasis on the experience of Black women in Brazilian society.

2   The artist's full name is Maria Auxiliadora da Silva, known as Maria Auxiliadora, as she will be referred to throughout the text.

3   Ana Elisa Lara Paulino, "O impacto do 'milagre econômico' sobre a classe trabalhadora segundo a imprensa alternativa," *Revista Katálysis*, v.23, n.3, 2020, pp.562-571.

4   According to Maria Cecília Felix Calaça, at weekends, Praça da República became a meeting point, initially on Saturdays and then on Sundays, when the event that became known as the Hippie Fair took place. It was later renamed the Art and Craft Fair.

5   It is important to highlight the relationship between Embu das Artes and political and artistic leaders who, among other topics, discussed the presence of the Black population, with people like Claudionor Assis Dias and Francisco Solano Trindade as references. See Maria Cecília Félix Calaça, *Movimento artístico e educacional de fundamento negro da praça da República: São Paulo 1960-1980*, Doctoral thesis (PhD in Brazilian Education) – Postgraduate Program in Brazilian Education, Federal University of Ceará, Fortaleza, 2013.

6   During this period, Maria Auxiliadora's work also had greater repercussions due to her contact with the art critic Mário Schenberg (1914-1990), who was decisive for her first solo gallery exhibition at the Mini Galeria USIS in 1970. See Adriano Pedrosa and Fernando Oliva (eds.), *Maria Auxiliadora: vida cotidiana, pintura e resistência*. São Paulo: MASP, 2018.

7   Petrônio Domingues, *Movimento Negro Brasileiro: alguns apontamentos históricos*. Tempo [online], v.12, n.23, pp.100-122, 2007.

8   The myth of racial democracy is a narrative that claims that racism does not exist in Brazil, claiming a supposed harmony between different racial groups due to miscegenation. Florestan Fernandes, in *A integração do negro na sociedade de classes: o legado da "raça branca"* (v.2, 5. ed. São Paulo: Globo, 2008), demonstrates how this ideology masks structural inequalities and power relations, and serves to maintain privileges and make it difficult to confront racism.

9   The terms "popular," "naif" and "primitive" have historically been used interchangeably to categorize artists on the margins of the hegemonic art system. Ludmila de Lima Brandão and Suzana Cristina Souza Guimarães ("Desconstruindo o Naif: a pintura de Alcides Pereira dos Santos," *Contrapontos*, v.12, n.3, pp.308-316, 2012) identify the term naif as a reproduction of colonial discourse, while Lilia Moritz Schwarcz in *A arte de despistar* (in Adriano Pedrosa e Fernando Oliva (eds.), *Maria Auxiliadora: vida cotidiana, pintura e resistência*. São Paulo: MASP, pp.96-106, 2018) demonstrates how these classifications naturalize cultural hierarchies. Renata Felinto, in "A ideia do Naif como estratégia decolonial" (in *Bienal de Naifs*. São Paulo: Sesc, 2021), proposes a decolonial re-reading of these terms, based on Krenak and Danto, where the naif emerges as a force of resistance and an expression of alternative cosmologies.

10　　　The Silva family consisted of eighteen siblings, many of whom were active in the popular fairs of Embu das Artes and Praça da República in São Paulo. Among the artists of the family were Sebastião Candido (1929–2016) and João Candido (1933) as draftsmen and painters; Vicente Paulo (1930–1980) in sculpture; Conceição Aparecida (1938) and Ilza Jacob (1946) in painting; Efigênia Rosário (1937) as storyteller; Natália Natalice (1948) in poetry; Georgina Penha (Gina) (1949) in painting and doll-making; and Benedito (1953–1998) as craftsman and painter.

11　　　Lélia Coelho Frota, *Mitopoética de 9 artistas brasileiros: vida, verdade e obra*. Rio de Janeiro: Funarte, 1978.

12　　　Renata Felinto, "Maria Auxiliadora: o pisar sensível, existências do invisível e visualidades do indizível," in *Maria Auxiliadora: vida cotidiana, pintura e resistência*. São Paulo: MASP, pp.32-40, 2018.

13　　　In 2003, Brazil passed Federal Law 10,639, which amends the Law on the Guidelines and Foundations of National Education and makes the teaching of Afro-Brazilian history and culture compulsory in the country's primary and secondary schools. The legislation aims to recognize and value the contribution of the Black population in shaping Brazilian society. As such, Maria Auxiliadora's work is a fundamental part of broadening discussions about the visual production of Brazil's Black population.

14　　　Renata Bittencourt, "Eu pinto crioulos," in Adriano Pedrosa and Fernando Oliva (eds.), *Maria Auxiliadora: vida cotidiana, pintura e resistência*. São Paulo: MASP, pp.32-40, 2018.

Memory Activated by Lived Experience, My Childhood, Gestures and Words

Keyna Eleison

MA CUM BA

A word that, when I was a child, was spoken quietly in the street and loudly in friends' backyards.

A word that was a smile among my family and a strange thing at school, a word that has taste, sound and people, smell and rhythm.

And on my way I came across macumba as a gathering, a power, a force, a school. And the shame I was taught to have lost its strength.

And with my eyes I listened, with my ears I listened, with my hands I listened, with my memory I listened.

I found something that, even though new, brought back memories of an entire relationship with the word and with the dynamics that the perception of macumba had taught me. I was present in something that connected me with so many affinities and so many new things. New and so external, strong and so everyday.

Because it was tradition, ecstasy, circles, drums.

Women with hands that command the wind, eyes that pierce time, and sound – that sound that pours out like a prayer, like a returning tide.

In Brazil, macumba is a word with weight and history. It is spoken with reverence, fear or disdain, depending on who is speaking and where they come from.

Deep down, macumba is sound, wood and leather in vibration, a name that came here in the wake of the pain of the kidnapping of nations, mixed with the languages of the margins, of those who were uprooted from their homes and had to rebuild their worlds.

Macumba is also a ritual, a force that beckons the invisible, that does not oppose chaos, but surrenders it to the sacred. It is dance, song, healing, but above all it is resistance, a celebration of spirituality, exuberance and abundance.

And there, on that Moroccan floor, I found myself facing something that seemed to come from the same construction, the same language.

The sounds and gestures were calling me.

Was this something new I recognized? Or was it another ancestrality, touching me with drums and strings that bear similar stories?

GNAWA

A breath. A word full of sea and desert.

Gnawa is music, but it is also a people. A people born from forced movements, from the scars of human trafficking, from the paths that Africa has traced between them.

The Gnawa, descended from the enslaved people of the Sahara, have found in music a way of remembering and continuing to live.

The Gnawa tradition is invocation, celebration and connection.

The guembri pulses with its strings, while the krakebs, with their small metal circles, click like a steady, rhythmic breath.

It is music for the body, for the spirit, to make you dance and to make you feel.

And in the sound, there are portals.

Gnawa rhythms are trance-like, opening up space for the invisible world to manifest, and so connections are made that overflow into dynamics of health, temporalities, blessings and collectivities. The human perspective is not constrained by the divine, it dissolves and sustains itself.

HADRA

An Arabic term meaning "presence," the ritual creates a safe and sacred space where participants can experience a profound connection with the divine. Sacred words are repeated, movements are repeated, sanctifying the moment. Through music and bodily movements, women enter a state of concentration and surrender, as if all the group's attention and energy converge to perceive the "presence" (Hadra) of God or the sacred in that instant.

A communal ritual of healing, seeking mystical ecstasy, and praising God, where the body functions as an instrument to experience and share the sacred dimension of life.

An intense spiritual experience mediated by music, chants, and dance.

Hadra and Gnawa are connected: they relate to mystical-musical practices in Morocco, often linked to Sufi brotherhoods or musical expressions seeking states of spiritual ecstasy. While each has its distinct characteristics, they share a common thread: the use of chants (zikr), rhythms, and dances that, through repetition, lead participants to a state of "presence" or trance, bringing them closer to a sacred dimension.

I saw women playing.

With agile hands and bodies taken by the music, they were rhythm and melody at the same time.

It was impossible to tell where the beats ended, and the dance began.

And from there, in the voices, movements and care, I saw macumba, *cambonagem*, circularity, joy, trance...

I saw people *cambonando*, being the mediators between the worlds. They carried pieces of cloth and attentive eyes, guiding the bodies of those who fell to the ground. And there, in that space that seemed like a temple, but also a celebration, saints were descending. Or were they ancestors?

Or simply, and transcendentally, a cure.

Ancient figures, of absolute strength, who entered bodies and transformed them.

In the circle, everything seemed connected, the present and the past.

They went to call me, I'm here. What's up?
They went to call me, I'm here. What's up?
That's where I came from, I came as a child, but I came as a child,
Someone warned me to tread this ground very lightly.
Someone warned me to tread this ground very lightly.

I brought Dona Ivone Lara here to keep me company in my thoughts. Because without macumba there is no samba, there is no healthy community body, community support, the thread that unites in voice and movement, the rhythm that recognizes itself as Black.

What is the distance between Gnawa and macumba?

Perhaps none at all.

Because both combine multiple perceptions in their rhythms, movements, singing and trance. Of the sacred that dances, of music that heals and beckons. They are languages that come from the path, the ground, the sweat, the earth, the ancestral cry that never falls silent.

In ecstasy, there are no distances. The sound, never to be contained, cuts through and flies. The guembri and the atabaque, distant relatives who recognize each other in vibration, a dialogue that crosses continents. The body that is *gira*, the *gira* that is body; it is the same body that delivers itself, to the saint, to the sound, to the singing. To the spirit, to what cannot be seen but can be felt. It is the same body that carries the memory of those who were torn away, those who crossed oceans and transformed pain and violence into music.

And I leave carrying the sound in my bones, the steps in my flesh, and the certainty of memories.

The sacred can have many languages, faces and names, and its essence is multiple; it doesn't come from the same seed, but from multiple connections. It is resistance and transcendence. It is movement and it shows us where we can still go.

Between the guembri and the drum, between the saints who descend and the ancestors who visit, the music continues.

It is all a force that does not bend, it is a bridge between worlds. And there, in that sound that still echoes, I understood that music is a pact of experience, of life.

That rhythms speak for us, even when words don't make sense. That the body that moves, in trance, is sacred territory, where the divine manifests itself in every turn, in every beat.

82

And if the guembri beckoned me, if the Gnawa sound pulled me to the center of the circle, it is because the drums from both here and there know that we are part of the same force. Made of music, of an unexplainable spirituality that guides and guards us.

And so I realize that the drum does not carry borders, but paths.

And that the trance, whether in Brazil or Morocco, is an act of remembering and being reborn; renewing and sustaining.

Pure affection, something I learned among my own people. Thank you.

83

Fatema U Trab / Fatima and the Dust:

A Musical Exploration of Gnawa Spirituality through Matrilineal Knowledge

Leila Bencharnia

This piece creates a space of profound listening, an homage to the unseen and the unspoken. It delves into the spiritual world of Gnawa tradition, rooted in Sufism and other African spiritualities, where music and rituals become pathways between the earthly and the divine. At its heart lies a tribute to the silent yet essential role of women – guardians of ancestral heritage, keepers of rituals, and weavers of the unseen threads that sustain their communities.

In Gnawa practices, nocturnal ceremonies unfold in rhythmic cycles, dissolving boundaries between time and spirit. While men often lead these rituals, it is women who preserve the deeper lineage, embedding their understanding into every gesture and creation. The loom becomes a powerful metaphor for this legacy: carpets, meticulously crafted, transform into maps of life, carrying encoded stories and spiritual truths passed through generations.

The soundscape of *Fatima and the Dust* draws from the improvisational essence of spiritual jazz, where polyrhythms echo the intricate interplay of weaving threads. Percussion vibrates with the pulse of hands shaping clay or stretching fabric, while tones intertwine fragments of memory and ritual. Silence weaves through the composition, creating space for reflection, amplifying the unspeakable, and inviting spiritual depths to emerge.

This work honors the unspoken strength and perception of women – their hands, their presence, and their silence – through which knowledge and tradition endure. It is an offering to the loom of existence, where sound and spirit, memory and rhythm are interwoven into a living tapestry. To listen is to step into this sacred weave, witnessing the matrilineal flow of life, resilience, and transformation.

Sound Piece

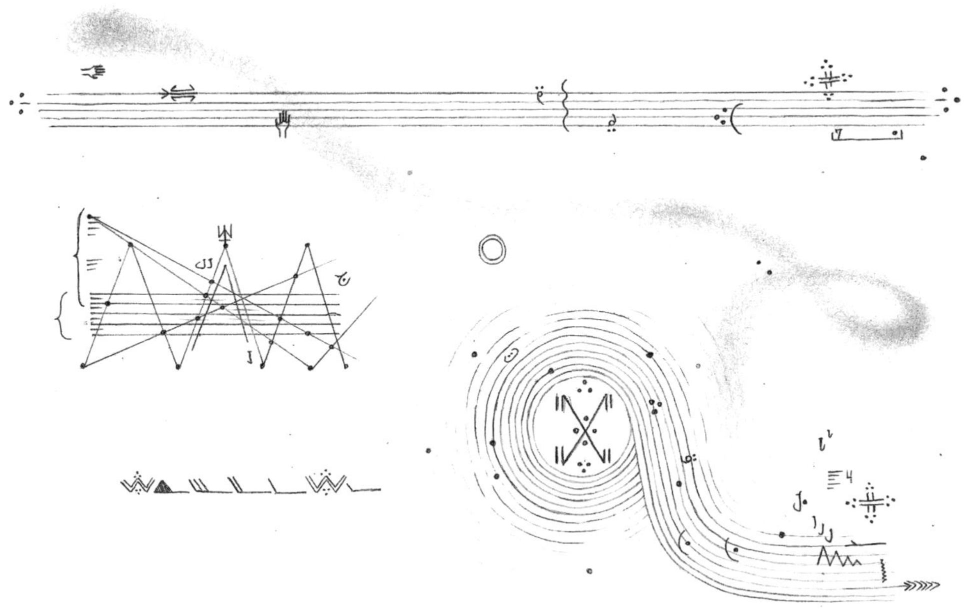

they speak in olive oil language and salty rhythm
        carpets are the sincerest place to read a story
the direction to avoid getting lost is to mecca and on the eleventh
        day I eat 7 dates

I will fast to learn to feel pain
I will learn the names of the cities they want to fool
        the ground grunts and the roots feel it
nothing will be like before nothing will be cancelled

children in Iraq
the scent of Lebanese trees the red sea of Yemen
the rhythms of Kilombo
The knit cotton of Burkina Faso the leaves of the Amazon

and the Andena land
they don't know that immortality is on the eleventh page of the
        Quran and you can't read it another Ramadan with
        za'atar between the fingers,
the tears among the diamonds silenced islands and hijabs
        on the 4 o'clock bus

free and the eternal song of Khartoum
        the women of the Atlas are free
free is the woman who walks every day in Pakistan
        the salt that cleanses fears is free

free are the ancestors who make the intention eternal through
        circular sounds free is the red dust of Palestine

"More Important Than the Work, the Journey": Listening and Storytelling as a Process

Amina Agueznay

Text developed from a conversation between the Fundação Bienal team and the artist on November 29, 2024.

Presence

I talk often about the intangible. That creates the tangible. About woven stories that produce the woven pieces. When I talk about woven, obviously, it could be anything. But woven stories, woven pieces. And to me, process.

So, if we talk about the intangible, we talk about process, ok? It's more important than the final work. I like building connections between projects. The thought process continues between an old project and a new one. They are constantly created and evolving. So I leave the door open for the project to evolve.

And the question is: when is a project, when is a work finished? Is it ever finished? For me, it is not. I hang it and I already see the next step, the next *fil conducteur*. And that's, for me, the intangible.

So, working with your hands is a slow process. Craft is a slow process. And this world is becoming faster and faster. We have to understand the process, to realize that it takes a long time to produce and install. And to understand what craft is. And that craft is also art. We often talk about craft as a bridge. But craft is art. End of conversation. And great, I'm good with that.

It's true. When does a piece of craft become a work of art? Is it in the atelier of the artisan when she makes it? Or is it in the gallery when it's hung and for the viewer to see? These are questions I ask myself. And if we talk about the intangible and the process, the workshops are, for me, mostly based on process.

And the process has to be an honest one, having an ethical approach, a mutual respect with people you work with, that involves listening to each other. Because when you listen, then there's magic. Then the energy that shines through is powerful, luminous. The energy radiating from the work.

I talk about presence. I don't talk about a piece of art or work of art as, "oh, it's beautiful." Does it have a presence? That's really more important than anything else. That's the intangible for me. And it also is palpable with all the senses. You know, it's seeing. Sometimes it's about hearing, touching, smelling. And what do I know? Eating, whatever.

In some remote areas, artisans still have the inheritance from their grandmother, great-grandmother, these piled up rugs and piled up covers. It's like a museum. The stories are there. So I did an installation where you have these piled up textiles. You read it immediately. That's the intangible becoming tangible. Because it's like, you know you know the story immediately, you read it.

Tabadoul

So I'm going to talk first about the artisans, the hands of the artisans. And then I'll tell a story about my hands. Because I think it's super important in the way I work. When I animate a workshop with artisans, and the restitution of the workshop is an installation for a show, watching the ladies or men, depending on the type of craft, work and listening to their stories, it reminds me maybe of the quilting process.
When you're sitting around a table you see all these people working individually for a common work and telling stories. And incredible stories that have nothing to do with the craft. So once trust is established, it's just incredible.

All the stories are woven to make one piece. But there are many, many, and they are quite incredible. The workshops, they're based on this mutual exchange.

We say *tabadoul* in Arabic. I'm learning from them and they're learning from me. And that's very important in my process. I never come in as "I'm the teacher, I'm teaching you." No, I mean, and that's baloney. It's not really what happens. We both learn. I learn all the time with them. I tell stories. The participants tell stories. And then I listen to them.

So once I tell my stories I usually show a presentation of a lot of images that are triggers for them. And then, let's say the next day, it's the hands-on. And I'm talking mostly about the weavers and the leathersmiths. The telling of the stories is through the workshops. And then they translate this with their hands.

But what's interesting is that, once I tell the stories, I give them felt-tip pens. And for example, for the rug weavers, I tell them, please draw me a rug. And they're like, I want to draw with my weaving, not with these pens. And when they start drawing, they're the most beautiful drawings. It's really incredible.

But what does it mean to listen? There are also silences during these workshops. But you still hear. What do you hear? You hear the hands weaving, punctuated by stories, of course, being told, gestures being corrected, senses being awakened, matters being touched, you know. And listening enables transmission. And that's really important for *la pérennité*, for continuity, for everything, for life, basically, to continue.

So I have some examples of two works. One is called *Skin* and one is called *Noise*. They are perfect examples to illustrate what I have just said. *Skin* is actually the first work that I did with the artisans. I was just starting, becoming an artist, you know. And a curator asked me if I could work with these women

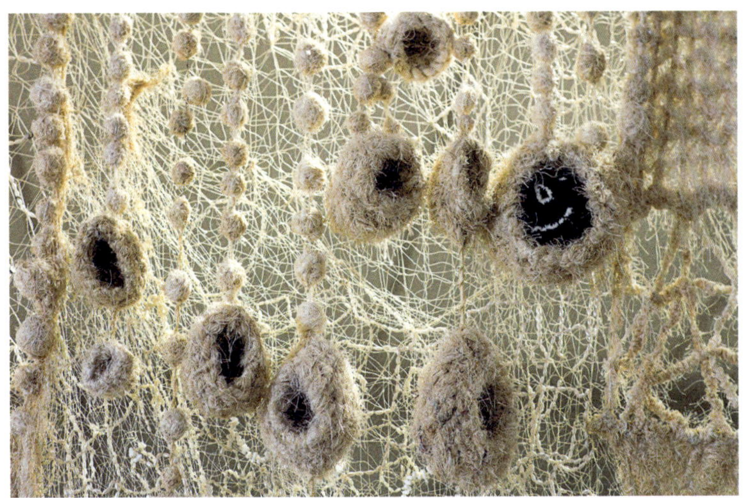

Skin, 2011. Installation composed of recycled fish net, viscose and nylon thread, cotton thread, sisal twine, stainless steel wire, plastic sequins, glass and plastic beads, paper, stainless steel structure; crochet, knitting, weaving, macramé, braiding, rope and pompom making, embroidery, randa, beading, sewing. 680 cm x 300 cm. Museum Mohamed VI of Modern and Contemporary Art, Rabat. Courtesy: Cultures Interface. Photo: Khalil Nemmaoui, 2016

artisans in Buznica. And originally it was a fisherman's village. There's some women there that are weavers and do crochet.

And so we used fishermen's nets. So there was this old fisherman, Bejani, may he rest in peace, who used to collect these used fishermen's nets. He and his wife would wash them. They would dry them and then I would take them. So process, I know now we talk about process. Because the work starts with the material. The story of the material itself. It's not just I go to a store and buy 10 kilos of fisherman's nets. No. And I

think that's really beautiful.

And after that, I made like a gigantic quilt, basically. The piece was called *Skin*. At that time, I was the chief of orchestra conducting. But I wasn't working. I was observing, directing, composing. But not working with my hands.

And with *Noise* it was not the case. *Noise* is an installation made out of wool. So Mohamed Benaissa[1] called me and he said, "I want you to animate a workshop with these ladies." You know, they do a little macrame, a little embroidery. "Can you do something?" I replied: "if I do something, it has to be a work that can be exhibited. I don't want to just make hats and bags and whatnot. I want to make a work."

So he agreed. And what was interesting in this process was that these ladies, if you give them wool, you know, immediately the material is linked to sweater. Even though this was wool for rugs. But still, sweaters, hats, functional things. And I was like, no, no.

And so I told them, "you make the matter with this material, but you don't make a hat." For example, this one woman, she's like, "I made this beautiful chicken." I said "ok, now you're going to behead the chicken." How to deconstruct this chicken? So she made three pom-poms. And I was like, "I like the pom-poms, but I don't like the chicken." So, well, we're going to kill the chicken. And I deconstructed the chicken. All of a sudden she had just this pom-pom. Then she started producing this pom-pom and creating her own matter. I thought that was really fabulous. So *Noise* was a co-creation.

And in this installation, you heard the voice of the ladies talking. Because they all had stories to tell. Unbelievable stories to tell while creating this. And I found this experience fascinating.

But then there's me. I tell stories with my hands too. For a while now, I started working with my hands again. It became important for me to experiment with my hands,

exploring new mediums, new techniques. It has become a regular practice.

Then I went to Madagascar in 2023. And I discovered raffia. So I started working with raffia. I started hand stitching, and I was so happy because that made me in balance within myself. For three weeks, I was this repetitive pattern, this gesture. I entered a meditative state. It was hypnotizing, and I loved it. I love the rhythm, the gesture of stitching on the raffia, and how this rhythm of the gesture regulates your own rhythm during the day. Because I worked nine hours. I didn't see the time.

So we were invited for this residency to do research on the work of Madame Zo. Madame Zo was a weaver.[2] She passed away because of Covid. She was a fabulous weaver. So from doing traditional weaving, she started experimenting. And she started introducing all kinds of stuff in her weavings. Video, films, bands. Anything she could find. I mean, plants, herbs, you name it, she wove it. Beautiful. So what I did is, basically, I took photos of details of the weaving.

And I started stitching them on the woven raffia that I bought in the local market. I started stitching these details. I had this urge. But in parallel to that, I worked with artisan embroiderers, weavers. It was fabulous.

What was really incredible is we were working in that space and there was always this butterfly that would come and stay on the weave, on Madame Zo's weaving. We would say, "that's Madame Zo." Her spirit is here with us. Madame Zo was a revelation. And transmission: her son is a weaver. He does beautiful work. He is a beautiful person. So there is an extension of Madame Zo in his hands.

She was incredible. She would like to go, get on the road with her weavings and stop wherever, you know, and show the work to anybody or everybody. I mean, what a fantastic way to make the art accessible. Because, well, people are intimidated to go in a gallery or in a museum. They will say, "no, it's not for me." Or they'll shy away. But when you get the art out on the street, then it's available for everybody. And people are being completely uninhibited. And I love that.

Bonds

My mother[3] was a student at the School of Fine Arts of Casablanca in the 1960s.[4] So she would take me with her on occasions, and I would play in the ceramics department with clay. I loved doing that. I was a hyperactive kid, so I also would run in the garden. I always had a ceramic tile in my hand, always. It was a playful period. I have screenshots of these moments that are at the school that are embedded in my mind still.

I remember Mohamed Melehi[5]. I loved him. Because I was little, but he was paying attention to me. He would take me to the ceramic studio. He would allow me to play with clay, he was attentive.

But I remember also mom taking me to Farid Belkahia's[6] atelier. At the time, mom didn't have her studio. And she needed a press. Farid had a press, so he told her, come and do your printmaking in the atelier.

Bert Flint[7] was a professor at the School of Fine Arts. May he rest in peace also. I remember his house, where he had these amazing glass cabinets where he had his collection of tribal jewelry, silver jewelry. That's when I was like, hey, look. Maybe that's where my interest started with jewelry. And the jewelry connected me then with the art installations and connected me with the artisans.

And the beautiful thing is: I was animating a workshop, a big program in Essaouira, where you had jewelers, silversmiths and woodmakers. I was commissioned to animate workshops for a year with artisans that create jewelry. And I met Bert Flint in Essaouira, in a center for the artisans, and I looked at him, and I'm an adult, he's not

93

young anymore, and I said, you're the reason why I'm here. We both looked at each other with a lot of emotions. And it made all the sense in the world.

You know, connecting the dots, that was something really powerful. So these are the people that I remember at the School of Fine Arts that had a huge impact. But not just what they did, but their universe, it was incredible for a child and a teenager. And all of them, they were great storytellers.

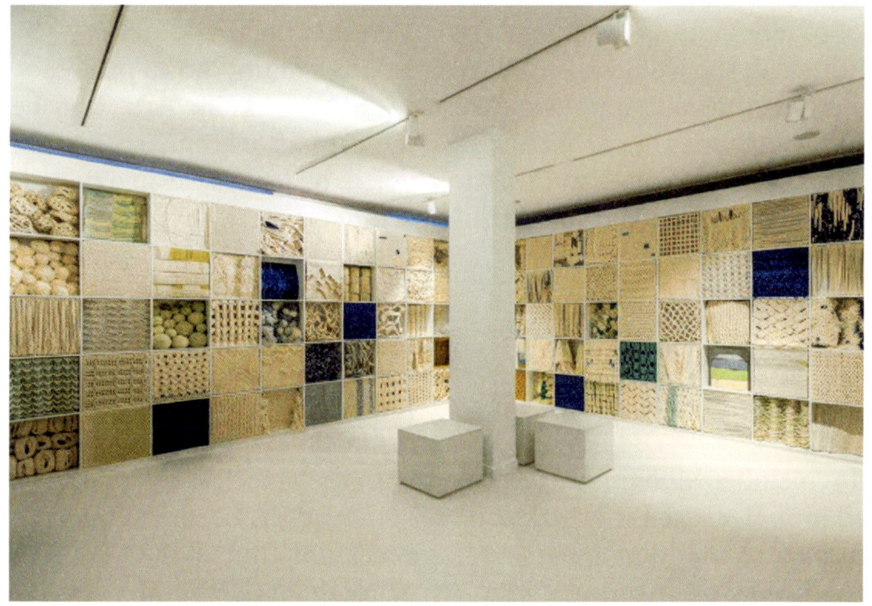

Amina Agueznay, *Noise*, 2018. Weaving, braiding, knitting, crochet, macramé, pompons, collage. Natural white and dyed wool, semi-precious stones, paper, metal and melamine faced mdf. 170 kg of wool. 210 boxes of 50 × 50 × 25 cm each. Museum of African Contemporary Art Al Maaden, Marrakech, 2019. © Saad Alami

Malika

If I go back to my mother, the house, when I think about it, it is filled with artwork. And like I said, my mom had this photo lab in the basement. And then she had an atelier where she had the printer. And she's a printmaker. And then, you know, that's where she paints. That's where I studied for my *baccalauréat*,[8] in her atelier. So, you see, they're all human. With their qualities and their flaws, and they die. And they're all pretty much gone now.

So I wanted to collaborate with my mother, I wanted to create memories inside her atelier. Her atelier is filled with great energy, where everything is possible. Where my mother is no longer my mother, but a peer helping another peer. And that's really very interesting. You take her out of the atelier, she's another person. And it's these territories, these worlds that are parallel. Because the atelier is in part of the house where she lives. So I wanted to continue a story. She's still working. And when you see this fragile woman taking the material for a monotype, preparing the color, and using the rolls to ink this material I gave her, it's very moving. She has her own world. That reminds me of the world of Farid. Not in the same way, or Melehi, or Bert Flint, or whoever.

They have that world that is still a true-blue world. And that's maybe why I keep on going back on the field all the time. Because to this day, I'm trying to understand why this interest in craft like this, why am I still collaborating, or having this participatory approach with craft? Why am I doing that still? And it's the people. And it's about people. More important than the work, the journey. And where am I going next? Where am I going next? You know, I don't know.

1   Mohamed Benaissa (1937) is a Moroccan politician. He was Morocco's Minister of Foreign Affairs and Culture. In 1978, together with the painter Mohamed Melehi, he invited artists to paint murals on the traditionally white walls of buildings in the city of Asilah, believing that art should not be limited to galleries. The Moussem d'Asilah, the official name of the Asilah Festival in Morocco, takes place every year and is now considered one of the most important festivals in North Africa.

2   Zoarinivo Razakaratrimo, known as Madame Zo (1956-2020), was an icon of the Madagascan art scene. Her work is characterized by the use of a wide range of natural and manufactured materials in dialogue with traditional Madagascan *lamba* weaving. Her textile works have unusual shapes and sizes, thanks to the looms she built herself, and integrate hundreds of materials such as newsprint, magnetic tape, electronic components, copper, bones, medicinal plants, industrial foam, rubber, wood shavings, or perishable food. Madame Zo died of Covid in 2020, and her work has been recognized worldwide since the 2000s.

3   For her contributions to modern art and abstraction in the history of Moroccan visual art, Malika Agueznay (1934) became internationally known as the first modernist woman artist in Morocco and a member of the experimental School of Fine Arts of Casablanca. From 1966 to 1970, Agueznay was the first woman to study at the Casablanca School, as it became known. In 1978, she took part in the first artists' workshop known as the Moussem d'Asilah, the Asilah Festival, where she became the first woman in Morocco to work with the technique of engraving.

4   The School of Fine Arts of Casablanca was founded in 1919 in Casablanca, Morocco. From the 1960s, under the direction of artists Farid Belkahia, Mohamed Melehi, and Mohamed Chabâa, it favored experimental and modernist approaches, teaching abstract art characterized by shapes, lines, geometric patterns, and primary colors typical of modernism. From 1964 to 1972, the school's practices aimed to promote the democratization of art studies and emphasized the use of traditional Moroccan crafts, both in the works produced and in the work of instructors on projects.

5   Mohamed Melehi (1936-2020), born in Asilah, was a Moroccan modernist artist and a central figure in the artistic movement centered around the School of Fine Arts of Casablanca. Between 1964 and 1969, Melehi taught painting, sculpture, and photography at the Casablanca School. At the time, the school was run by Farid Belkahia, with whom Melehi would form the Casablanca School movement. In 1969, Melehi and his colleagues from the school, including Farid Belkahia, Mohamed Chabâa, and others, organized an exhibition-manifesto entitled *Présence Plastique* [Plastic Presence]. The artists exhibited their works at the Jemaa el-Fna, a famous street

market in the medina of Marrakech, in opposition to an "official Moroccan art" salon taking place at the same time. *Présence Plastique* is considered the founding moment of modernism in Morocco.

6	Farid Belkahia (1934-2014) was a Moroccan education reformer and modernist artist. He served as director of the School of Fine Arts of Casablanca from 1962 to 1974, during the period of the modernist movement of the School of Fine Arts of Casablanca. As an artist, he worked mainly with painting, metalwork, and leather.

7	Born in Holland, Bert Flint (1931) has lived in Marrakech since 1957, where he has researched different aspects of Berber culture and collected objects and fragments for over sixty years. From 1965 to 1968, he taught art history at the School of Fine Arts of Casablanca and took part in the modernist movement with the other artists mentioned in this article.

8	A national diploma certifying the completion of secondary education in France. It is required for admission to higher education, providing access to both university studies and professional training.

97

Artisans of Rupture or Renewal?

Fatima-Zahra Lakrissa

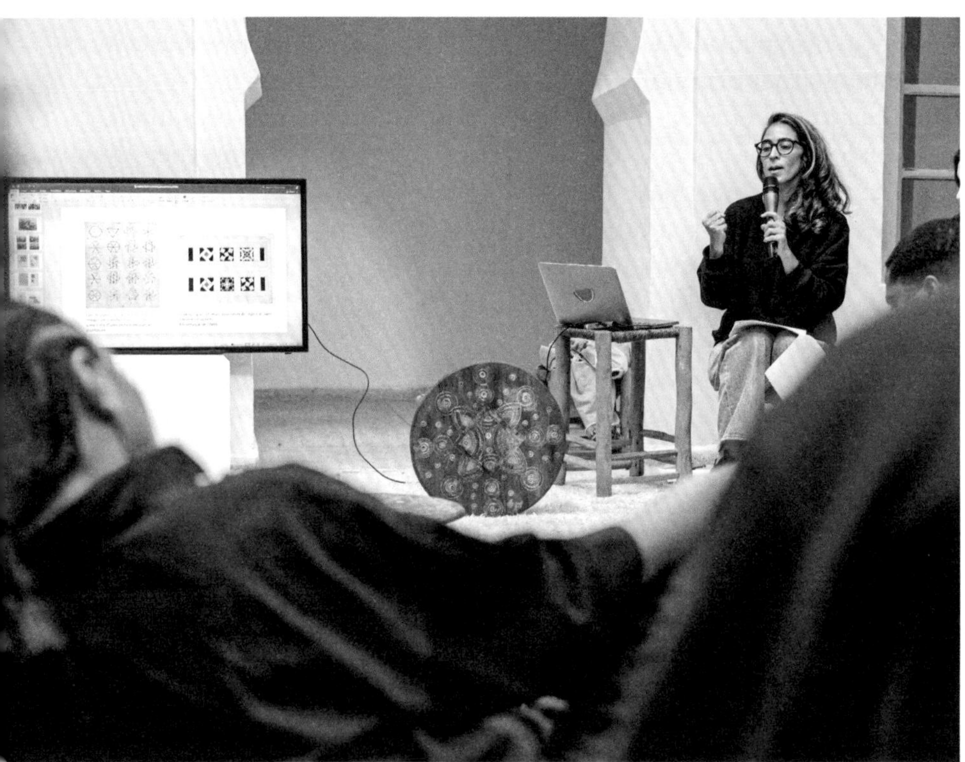

All photos: © Youssef Boumbarek /
Fundação Bienal de São Paulo

The traditional Houdrane carpet is decorated on a background of horizontal and vertical lines forming more or less regular squares. At the bottom of the carpet opposite, that is to say at the beginning of the weaving of this piece, the artist committed several transgressions. He or she decided to adapt the traditional grid to his or her personal expression. Twice he or she removed a horizontal line and interrupted one of the vertical lines, thereby creating spaces that offered him or her the possibilities of expression that he or she needed.

Bert Flint, "Légendes et commentaires Bert Flint," *Horizons maghrébins-Le droit à la mémoire*, n. 22, 1994, p.44.

Folk art is generally characterized as decorative because certain elements that originally had a dynamic meaning, once degraded and emptied of their original meaning, automatically remained, transformed and reused in unlimited combinations. In other cases, it was the apparent simplicity of the forms that led the viewer, unable to read the content, to see a single, seemingly decorative dimension, whereas in reality there was a series of values expressed and contributed to by the manufacturer and his customers.

Toni Maraini, "Considérations générales sur l'art populaire au Maroc," *Maghreb Art*, n. 2, 1966, pp.10-12.

Propaganda, which until now had been mainly verbal, has already produced the most encouraging results [...]. A private workshop in a major inland town [...] has built up a clientele that does not give it a moment's rest. Berber carpets from another workshop on the coast featured prominently in several of Paris' most famous department stores. [...] This kind of recognition shows that the general public is far from indifferent to efforts that began in Morocco, and more particularly in the Department of Indigenous Arts.

Prosper Ricard, *Corpus des tapis marocains*, II, Tapis du Moyen-Atlas, 1926.

The French protectorate at the beginning of the 20th century led inevitably to a confrontation between traditional and popular Moroccan art and the disciplines of anthropology and art history, which later became the subject of exploration at the School of Fine Arts in Casablanca in the 1960s. From the exploration of the two disciplinary confrontations at the Casablanca School emerged a distinctive constellation of personalities and approaches. The first – associated entirely with the figure of Prosper Ricard – raised questions about the key issues of safeguarding, prioritizing, and musealizing artistic productions that were referred to as Indigenous arts or craftmanship. For the second, a trio of artists comprising Farid Belkahia, Mohamed Melehi, and Mohammed Chabâa were key. This group of artists alone symbolizes the reform of art education that occurred in the wake of Moroccan independence and the transformation of the artistic arena, which increasingly embraced the social sphere by addressing its problems and questions. This group of artists alone symbolizes the reform of art education that occurred in the wake of Moroccan independence and the transformation of the artistic arena, which increasingly embraced the social sphere by addressing its problems and questions. After a long period of academic and almost purely technical teaching, the Casablanca School of Fine Arts reoriented itself towards a multidisciplinary program thanks to Farid Belkahia, its director from 1962 to 1974. Belkahia implemented his reform project by bringing together a teaching team made up of artists Mohamed Melehi and Mohammed Chabâa, Together, they introduced innovative teaching methods, focused on experimentation in the workshop, research on Arabic calligraphy and traditional and popular arts, mobilization for the integration of art in architecture and public space, and many other artistic and political positions aimed at structuring the Moroccan artistic field and its dialogue with pan-Arab and pan-African artistic networks. They introduced innovative teaching methods, focused on experimentation in the workshop, research on Arabic calligraphy and traditional and popular arts, mobilization for the integration of art in architecture and public space, and many other artistic and political positions aimed at structuring the Moroccan artistic field and its dialogue with pan-Arab and pan-African artistic networks. Accompanied by the theoreticians Toni Maraini and Bert Flint, these artists initiated the creation of the journal *Maghreb Art* (1965–1969), which set out the methodological and theoretical principles for the rehabilitation of the traditional and popular arts of Morocco.

101

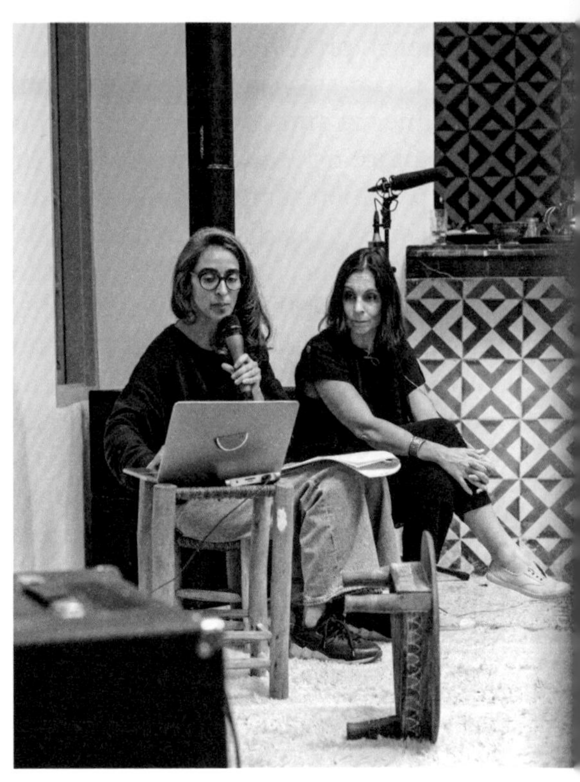

Stagings and Narratives

As the director of the Service des Arts Indigènes (1920–1935) and, subsequently, its honorary director, Prosper Ricard was the architect behind the heritage policy applied to local artistic production. Its goal was the renewal, resurrection, and revitalization of Moroccan crafts, which were considered threatened due to the presence of the colonial power and its economic and social influence on Moroccan life. Ricard took on the role of savior of the country's crafts, which he sought to define and recreate through the prism of authenticity and pure form.[1] The fabrication of authenticity was based on an ethnographic diagnosis of selective interpretations of heritage and methods of inventorying and categorizing traditional artistic practices. Technical drawing played an important role, as evidenced by his notes and numerous sketchbooks relating to his research on various artistic forms of North Africa.[2]

Immediately after its creation, the Service des Arts Indigènes undertook extensive campaigns to collect traditional works, or at least those labeled as such, to be exhibited in the newly created museums of Indigenous arts, which housed the first ethnographic collections.[3] A first distinction was made between crafts and arts according to

102

their function; a second one between the arts described as "rural" or "Berber" and "urban art." The former, linked to a family production structure, are characterized by geometric forms; and the latter are structured around professional bodies and feature floral motifs.[4] This distinction served as an argument in Ricard's claim that the colonial administration had discovered and attributed a heritage and market value to those artistic productions – mainly, the rural carpets. His graphic and stylistic studies of Moroccan carpets culminated in a number of publications, the best-known of which is the four-volume *Corpus des tapis marocains* (1923-1934).[5]

In the process of safeguarding and modernizing the production of carpets, technical innovation was the essential argument. It was linked to the idea of progress and the appropriate evolution of forms, giving the subject a new centrality in the imaginary vision of change they wanted to forge. Ricard's aim was to reveal the "initial pattern" common to carpets, grouped into categories according to the regions where field research was carried out. The State stamp, established by the protectorate administration, was the official mark of authenticity, the criteria for which were defined in the *corpus*. It was supposed to preserve the image and prestige of the Moroccan industry and to guard against possible aesthetic and stylistic deviations. These processes of patrimonialization facilitated the emergence of an essentialist vision of traditional Moroccan arts, whose aesthetic value, in the eyes of the colonial authorities, was based on the ahistorical character of a purely formal, even mechanical, ornamental grammar.

Maghreb Art: A Counter-patrimonial Model?

Following Moroccan independence in 1956, aesthetic and moral considerations made their way into the appraisal of local artistic productions. Their emergence at the School of Fine Arts of Casablanca in the mid-1960s played a key role in the birth of abstraction rooted in the secular artistic tradition. The journal *Maghreb Art* accompanied the plastic experiments performed by the trio Farid Belkahia, Mohamed Melehi, and Mohammed Chabâa with theoretical research aimed at renewing the discourse on artisans. Under the editorial direction of Belkahia, and with the participation of Bert Flint, Toni Maraini, and Melehi, who was also the director of graphic design, *Maghreb Art* bears witness to the first attempts to structure a new field of knowledge between artistic and ethnographic experimentation, material culture, and art history.

103 The first issue was commissioned by the Centre Marocain pour la Recherche Esthétique et Philosophique, founded in Marrakech in 1963 by Bert Flint. Issues two and three were published by the School of Fine Arts of Casablanca. The first two issues (Fall 1965 and Fall 1966) included texts by Flint and Maraini. The third issue (Spring 1969) contained no text; in addition to notes on Melehi and Chabâa's studios, it presented a previously unpublished photographic archive of the so-called "decorative pictorial productions" discovered by Flint on the ceilings of the zaouias in the Souss region and then photographed by Melehi. The study of a *corpus* of so-called traditional and popular art objects outlined the contours of a new imaginary of change, enabling popular creativity to be given greater attention and symbolic effectiveness in this endeavor to rehabilitate the arts in Morocco.

The advocacy of local artistic sources was supported by Flint's research in visual anthropology. His knowledge, patiently acquired through fieldwork, was formalized through the study of crafts and techniques and socio-ethnographic research. His studies focused mainly on the carpets of the Haouz region, on jewelry (mainly from the Drâa Valley), the mosques from the Nfis Valley with their engraved columns, and on the painted ceilings in the mosque in the village of Aït Ouajaj (Imdentaguen, High Atlas).[6] They shed new light on the relationship between the rural and the urban and their respective links to social and artistic life in Morocco, as revealed by Flint, to demonstrate the descent of rural art from the Maghreb and Amazigh traditions.[7]

The research carried out by Bert Flint, who had lived in Morocco since 1957, intersects with the theoretical concerns of Toni Maraini, who arrived in the country in 1962 with the desire to pursue her studies on popular arts in the Moroccan and Afro-Mediterranean context. Her research on popular art contributed to the development of a discourse on heritage that drew on the logic of the mixture of different cultures, consolidated by theses of trans-Mediterranean cultural transfers in the sphere of archaeology and prehistory,[8] which informed her thinking, as well as the course on art history courses she taught at the school from 1965 to 1969.[9] During those years, Maraini's teaching was enriched by Flint's devoted study of the traditional and popular arts. Flint and Maraini shared a desire to broaden horizons beyond the European sphere and to restore a formerly neglected art history that was open to artistic expression. Bert Flint based his analyses of objects on a linguistic model – that of the grammar of forms and symbols – while Toni Maraini sought to construct a field of knowledge around the objects of material culture at the crossroads of art and anthropology.

104

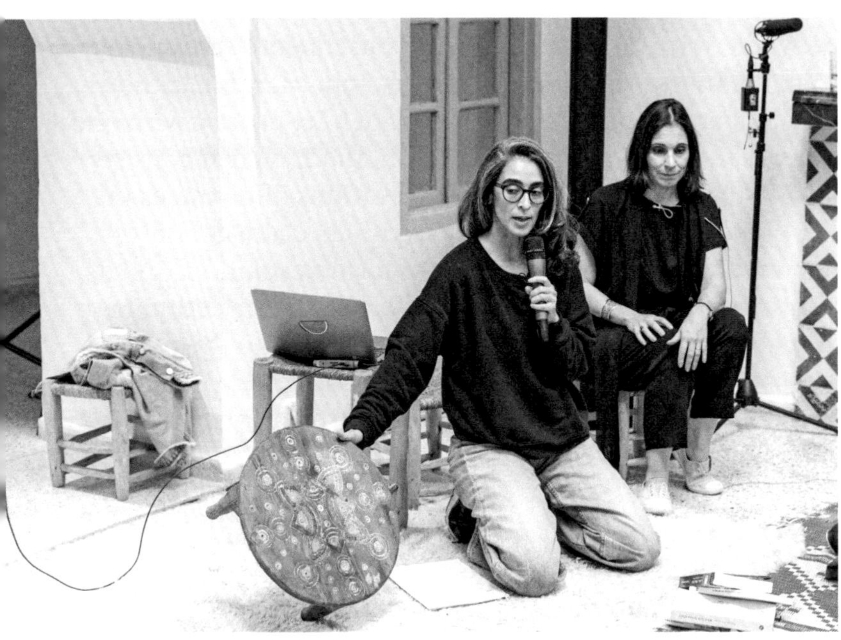

At the Crossroads of Disciplines

Between Flint and Maraini, the question was not simply one of substance but also of method. This led to Maraini's condemnation of Bert Flint's two-part model of "form and symbol" in his article "Forme et symbole du bijou marocain. Un problème de parahistoire" [Form and Symbols in Moroccan Jewelry: A Parahistorical Problem], published in *Intégral* in 1974.[10] Their opposition was based on methodological and disciplinary differences in the application of anthropological tools to traditional and popular art objects.

While Flint sought to isolate, that is, magnify, the specific symbolism of a form, Maraini constantly conditioned the history of forms on political, religious, social, and – above all – historical data. Maraini's critique goes beyond the case of Flint. It is applicable to a considerable part of Western thought, which at the time was dominated by the linguistic model that advocated the autonomy and supremacy of the signifier.[11] More fundamentally, for Maraini, it was a matter of defending the foundations of a practice that was emerging in Morocco – a post-ethnological art history that she wanted to inscribe simultaneously in a process of critical reflection and link with anthropology.

105 For Bert Flint, forms play an essential role, since they are the only evidence of culture when written documents and, consequently, chronological elements are lacking. In the face of this absence, Toni Maraini acknowledges the contribution of anthropology, which provides art history with one of its principal conceptual tools, the "comparative method," which consists in reconstructing a missing object from cross-observations of its traces in existing objects. Bert Flint's discourse on objects, with its claims to universality, its fascination with the internal principles of form's evolution, and its subjective interpretations, seemed closer to a nineteenth-century ethnology than to the critical modernity Maraini wished to introduce into the field of art. Her critical approach, with its conceptual caution and rejection of reductionism and essentialism, seems to be in line with that of the critical modernity of the first half of the twentieth century, from which she drew her inspiration.[12]

The debate over popular and traditional arts reflects the complexity of a historical situation whose issues are not limited to the 1960s, but resonate throughout the cultural destiny of post-independence Morocco to the present day. Two forces are intertwined: the overthrow of Western values on the one hand, and the development of a process of critical reflection on the other, expressed in the fields of literature, history, poetry, and sociology with fundamental contributions from other French-language cultural magazines such as *Souffles* (1966–1972), *Intégral* (1971–1977) and *Lamalif* (1966–1988).

1   The personal archives of Prosper Ricard in the Oudayas Library, Rabat. On the activities of Prosper Ricard and the organisation of the Service des Arts indigènes, see Muriel Girard, "Invention de la tradition et authenticité sous le Protectorat au Maroc: L'action du Service des Arts Indigènes et de son directeur Prosper Ricard," *Socio-anthropologie*, v.9, n.19, 2006.

2   Prosper Ricard highlighted the contribution of the works of Jules Bourgoin, French architect and theorist of ornament. See Jules

Bourgoin, *Les Éléments de l'art arabe: le trait des entrelacs*. Paris, Firmin-Didot, 1879; and *Études architectoniques et graphiques: mathématiques, arts d'industrie, architecture, arts d'ornement, beaux-arts*. 2 v. Paris: C. Schmid, 1899-1901, in Habiba Aoudia, *Les "Feuillets d'art" de Prosper Ricard. Inventaire et analyse du fonds Prosper Ricard du musée du quai Branly*, 2014.

3   On the Musée Colonial's missions and their role in colonial cultural policy, see Habiba Aoudia, "La fabrique du musée d'art marocain: l'œuvre de Prosper Ricard," *L'Année du Maghreb*, v.19, pp.37-53, 2018.

4   Jean Baldoui, "Quelques étapes de l'artisanat marocain," *Bulletin de l'Association Populaire des Amis des Musées* (*A.P.A.M.*), July 1941. Fonds Prosper Ricard, batch 738, in the Prosper Ricard collection (part of the Service des Beaux-Arts, des Antiquités et des Monuments Historiques, transferred to the Archives du Maroc, Rabat. See also Muriel Girard, 2006, op. cit.

5   Prosper Ricard, *Corpus des tapis marocains*, 4 v. Casablanca, 1923-1934.

6   Bert Flint, *La culture afro-berbère de tradition néolithique saharienne en Afrique du nord et dans les pays du Sahel*. Marrakech: Editions Jardin Majorelle, 2018, pp.330-331.

7   Bert Flint, "Culture populaire, culture d'élite," in Bert Flint, *Forme et symbole dans les arts du Maroc. v. 2: Tapis, Tissages*. Tangiers: E.M.I., 1974.

8   A review of Moroccan archaeology from 1961 to 1964 presents the results of studies and discoveries made in the pre- and protohistoric, Roman, and pre-Islamic periods, showing the history of the Mediterranean through the prism of a very distant cultural mix. See *Bulletin d'archéologie marocaine*, v.5 Tangiers: Musées et Antiquités du Maroc, 1964. See also Germaine Tillion, *Le Harem et les Cousins*. Paris: Editions du Seuil, 1966, p.87, which Toni Maraini references in "Mémoires métissées. Le paradigme antique," *Insaniyat*, n. 32-33, pp.25-38, 2006.

9   Toni Maraini, "Réflexions autour d'un cours d'histoire de l'art" [1990], in Toni Maraini, *Écrits sur l'Art*. Casablanca: Le Fennec, 2014, pp.259-284.

10   Toni Maraini, "Forme et symbole du bijou marocain. Un problème de parahistoire," *Intégral*, n. 7, January 1974, pp.22-25. The year 1974 also saw the publication of Bert Flint's *Tapis et Tissages*, which followed *Bijoux, amulettes* (1973), devoted to the subject of "Forme et symbole dans les arts du Maroc," introduced in 1967, with the exhibition of the same title held at the school's La Coupole gallery in the Parc de la Ligue Arabe.

11   Ibid., p.23.

12   This approach is corroborated by contemporary references to other anthropologists such as the UK's Edmund R. Leach. Leach and his *Critique of Anthropology*, 1968: an anthology of writings published between 1943 and 1959 whose self-critical dimension made it attractive. Ibid., p.25.

I Write on Cloth for Those Who Can't Read

Alberto Pitta

Text developed from a conversation between the Fundação Bienal team and the artist on November 14, 2024.

Beto

I was a child who caused a lot of trouble. I was always very curious. My childhood was during the dictatorship. So I'm from the 1960s, I was born in 1961. You kind of live and breathe, even as a child, a little bit of what's going on. Even from the news that reached our home. It was a time when you realized that it was very different and everything was very controlled – everyone knew everything, even your every step. So I can measure that time by the way I was brought up, and I didn't understand it, because when I came home my parents already knew if I'd been out on the street, where I'd been, what I'd done, if I'd eaten at someone's house, if I'd had a fight.

It was that African saying that a child is raised by an entire neighborhood.[1] And that came to make sense to me because I remembered that in the old days, in working-class neighborhoods, you were raised not only by your family, but by the baker, the butcher, the shopkeeper, the lady from the haberdashery, the guy from the store, everyone knew whose children they were. So they'd pass by and say "look, that's the son of Mr. Eduardo, who has a workshop in such and such a place." In other words, there was a kind of concern for other people's children.

In my adolescence, I really wanted to be a soccer player, I always say that. I thought it was possible. And it was,

really. I was a goalkeeper, I trained with teams here in Salvador, and I was particularly passionate about Esporte Clube Ypiranga, because I had a cousin who was a referee and Ypiranga supporter. He was from Cachoeira, where my mother's family comes from. My grandfather was a teacher in this town in the Recôncavo region of Bahia. I later learned that Ypiranga was a team founded here in Salvador in 1916 so that Black people could play soccer. I used to train with that team. They say I was good at it.

I think Carnival was stronger for me. So I became interested in the *blocos* and cinema. In other words, I liked everything that we could actually have access to. First, with my older brothers. And then later on my own initiative, always wishing to be in places because I'd heard about them. I grew up listening to Dorival Caymmi. In the second half of the 1960s, I had a sister who played the accordion. She would come home at night with her friends and play music. We were privileged to have access to these things. At the same time, we understood the changes of the generals. In short, we were understanding how Brazil worked as a political system, as a system of government.

I was interested in all these things, but very much in the aesthetics of Carnival. And then, in 1974, Ilê Aiyê came along. One of my brothers, Alísio Pitta, was a friend of the guys from Liberdade.[2] So he would bring home the news from 1973, 1974, 1975, about these movements. And the music thing too, because every self-respecting house had a garage with a stereo, or the living room was bigger than the other rooms, because the living room was for dancing. So all of this,

the Afro cultural movements of the 1970s, we were part of that, of this political interest. I come from that place.

I'm a man who pays attention to everything. For example, here in the studio there's a little plaque that says Faculdade da Atenção [Faculty of Attention]. That's where I was trained, paying attention, as a street

Print created by Alberto Pitta based on a drawing by Mãe Santinha, an ialorixá and the artist's mother, a seamstress and embroiderer known for her intricate embroidery and richelieu work. The original artwork was adapted for screen printing.
Courtesy of the artist

corner social scientist. Everything interests me. I learn about everything. That's my background and the background of my work.

It's these things of the imagination that are so much better than anything else. Better than the dream itself. So I'm imagining all the time. When I'm making a float, for example, I don't draw a line. I obtain everything and assemble it. So whoever is working with me has to feel that. Sometimes I think of a piece diagonally and the guy takes it and places it horizontally. It looks better than I'd thought of it. So let's take it from there. Because it all has to be construction. Of course you design it, you label it, but when you're making it, that's when it starts to emerge. That's the soul of the thing, the soul of the work and the art is precisely there. It's when the other person comes along and puts something on top of that giant thing you've made. When he puts that in, he's in it. And a lot of people will be in it too.

My art is just like that. I don't have the slightest problem with someone coming along and saying why don't you do this, this, and this. It's like looking at a work of art and saying you don't understand it. When you say you don't understand it, that's the best result, because you've thought about it. It's not just a case of arriving and looking at a work that no longer belongs to the artist.

He put it there, it's not his anymore, it's gone. Now it belongs to the viewer. And those who see it are the ones who are going to interpret it for themselves.

1981

I actually learned silkscreen first, I didn't even say "screen printing". Right away, I liked the magic of printing, and I didn't know how it was all done. It was the first real access. I started working with a guy called José Ribamar, who made the coats of arms for school uniforms in Salvador. He would travel to inland Bahia, or even Sergipe, and take those schools run by priests, and arrive in Salvador: "let's do this, three thousand coats of arms for a school." Think of it, three thousand coats of arms, each with five colors. My God, there were 15,000 prints. So I picked it up, because he printed very quickly.

And then I learned how to print, because I made the shirt, you bought the coat of arms at the school and sewed it onto the shirt, turning it into a pocket. So you made five thousand small coats of arms. You had to cut them out, you had to mark them and cut them out, in a fabric like tergal, you know. It was a grueling job. But that's exactly where

I learned how to do it, because that was the silk-screen technique.

And, as Afro and Afoxé *blocos* emerged and this movement took off in Salvador, people started calling me to make their costumes. First to make what they already had in mind, because, as I mastered the silkscreen technique, I could make the matrices and print them. Then I said, no, now I'm going to do it.

Then they started giving me the theme and the responsibility of creating the print for the *bloco*. So it was all very localized. You'd get a *bloco de índio*,[3] and it would be a mask, the hem of the pants, the vest, the jacket. So it was localized printing, it wasn't run-of-the-mill printing. I started creating for various groups and I didn't even realize, I thought it was a group of 50, 100, and when I got there, there were a thousand people. I'm like, wow, and I did it. It was a time when we didn't keep things.

Gathering of Experiences

Fabric is my platform for discussion. It's not even a speech, it's a discussion. In cloth I see precisely this metaphor of possibilities, of talking about various issues. On the other hand, cloth means clothing. Cloth was what my mother would go out to buy in the Baixa dos Sapateiros[4] and bring home and cut up for us. We didn't have ready-made clothes. She made pants and shirts herself. She took measurements and made everything for everyone. But they were always cold colors, so to speak. It was navy blue, khaki, brown, gray. Those were the colors we wore at the time. I didn't particularly like them, but we had to wear them. That's what we had.

But she tried to do her best with those colors. So much so that today I work a lot with earthy tones, and I always remember those colors. Because they were colors that made you stand out as little as possible. They were colors that didn't attract attention. My parents related this precisely to the period of dictatorship. A time when Black people didn't wear green, red, yellow, or prints. No way. So when you wore those tones, brown, khaki, navy blue, it was a way of camouflaging yourself, of protecting yourself.

And we understood this gradually. But then, with the *blocos*, their colors, the boldness we saw in people, with the emergence of Ilê Aiyê, and this discourse through the cloth, the aesthetics, I got involved. And the fact that I realized that a lot of the people who come out of these groups don't know how to read, haven't had the opportunity to go to school, I started writing on the costumes, adding things to provoke those who don't know how to read.

Because can you imagine someone wearing an Ilê Aiyê, Muzenza, Cortejo Afro, Olodum costume[5] and not being able to read? It's a costume full of stories, but he can't read. And he notices that everyone is reading what is literally written on the cloth, except for him. Of course, we can't measure this, but somehow this person will start to want to learn to read because of this, because he's been provoked the whole time at Carnival. So he'll leave Carnival with a lack, which is precisely this, of interest in what's written on his costume. So it was by observing this that I began to tell the story on the costumes of the *blocos*. So there always has to be writing, whatever it is.

Beyond symbols, signs, in short, semiotics, you write. And that thing I always talk about when meeting illiterate people, because even those who come from else-where, who come from academia, who had the opportunity to go to school, will arrive at an Afro *bloco* and won't be able to understand the float, won't be able to understand the attire of the king and queen, won't understand the cloth, won't be able to read the symbols that attracted them. And he'll ask the guy next to him, who can't read, and who will tell him a whole story. And then, automatically, people identify themselves. The people who go out in the Afro *blocos* go out seeking to identify themselves, they have a motivation to go out in these *blocos*.

It's these stories that we gather and, somehow, put on the cloth, writing, telling, cutting, sewing, thinking about the other person; who needs to like the clothes, like the detail, who needs to understand that care has been taken, because the hem is well done and everything, the fabric is well printed, it arrived beautiful, colorful, and people will look beautiful, because people want, at the end of the story, to recover their energy through the techniques. There's no point in treating poverty with poverty. It's no use. You have to do your best for the people. So that's the logic.

People take it home and it becomes a cushion, it becomes a tablecloth, it becomes a table runner, it goes into a frame, it goes on the wall, it becomes a curtain. That's identification with cloth. So it's another kind of commitment. I know about this other commitment.

Carnivals

Along with the *bloco*, there's a whole movement beyond Carnival. There's the music, for example, and the responsibility of translating the entity's thinking into a parade. In other words, it's a school, where you are constantly learning about events, adversities, and differences of opinion within an organization, which is normal today, and which was very common and happened a lot back then. There wasn't much information for anyone. So it was a free and sovereign Bahian Africa embroidered on the drawing boards of the imagination. We imagined a free and sovereign Africa.

At the time, there was also Malê de Balê.[6] We were curious about it and then the story of the Malês came to us. The Malês Revolt, of January 25, 1835. Everything was imaginary. We would imagine everything. In other words, it was a big screen of imagination, and we watched the movies. The movies were the Búzios Revolt, the Malês Revolt, the liberation of African countries, colors, signs, symbols, aesthetics, struggles. This movie was on everyone's mind in the city. And, above all, those who made art in the *blocos*.

It was interesting to do a carnival with a Muslim theme. It's also a question of the aesthetics of Muslims, of the Tuaregs, for example, who have that kind of turban that goes over their heads, that they roll up... Because it's there to protect them from the heat. So much cloth in the desert is precisely to protect you against the heat. If you don't have anything in the desert, you'll be fried to death. The cloth protects you.

Returning to the story of Malê de Balê, one year they put a battle tank on the street, and they drove down Praça Castro Alves. The float was a tank. And the whole Malê de Balê band were dressed as guerrilla fighters. And the city stood still, watching. And the *bloco* came down, exalting the Malês, the Malês Revolt of 1835, and hyper empowered, dressed in Pan-Africanist color. The guys came together, a colorful, beautiful, African thing. These are things that leave their mark.

At the Olodum Carnival in 1990, the theme was "From the Sahara Desert to the Brazilian Northeast." I dressed everyone in black. And everyone watched and imagined everything in black and white, in an extremely colorful Carnival. Of course, the press was hard on it, the revelers wanted to beat me up inside the *bloco*, they looked at me: "What kind of costume is that?" But it was the José Sarney government, a period of terrible inflation, of lack of money.

Then, the next day, the press said: "it's because Olodum is protesting against inflation." The press embraced it, everyone embraced it, but I almost got beaten up on Friday. Gal Costa even recorded the song "Revolta Olodum" on the *Plural* album (1990). "Ô Curisco, Maria Bonita sent for you." It's these provocations that the Afro *bloco* gives us.

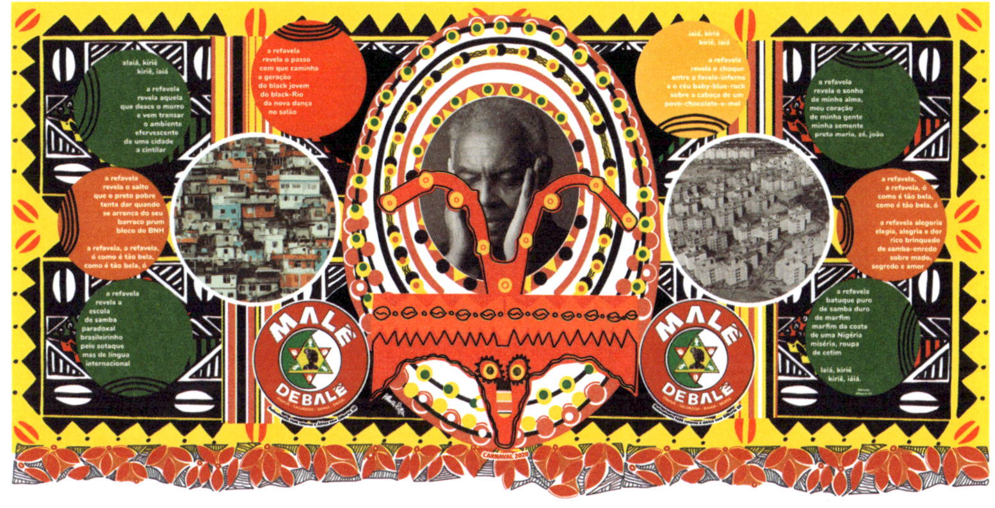

Print for the Malê de Balê *bloco*, 2019
Courtesy of the artist

Mãe Santinha and the Instituto Oyá

My mother always worked in the field of education, in addition to playing the piano and speaking French. From an early age, she taught her older siblings. One of them, Dr. Carmelito da Rocha Pitta, who passed away a few years ago, became a doctor and hospital director in São Paulo. She was the one who taught him to read and write before he left Bahia to move to São Paulo and start a family. This is important because her concern for children has been present in her life since childhood.

Those that nobody wants, those that nobody takes on. I'm talking about the state and the municipality, above all. And with this tradition of always welcoming children into our homes, we ended up founding the Instituto Oyá.

Then we realized that we needed to continue her efforts. And the Instituto is here, in the neighborhood of Pirajá, which is an important neighborhood, which also tells a bit about the Independence of Bahia, the 2nd of July. There's a pantheon, a church, General Labatut is buried there, and a whole history here in the neighborhood. Apart from the great Bacia do Cobre, which is an everyday sight for us. And a little further on, the

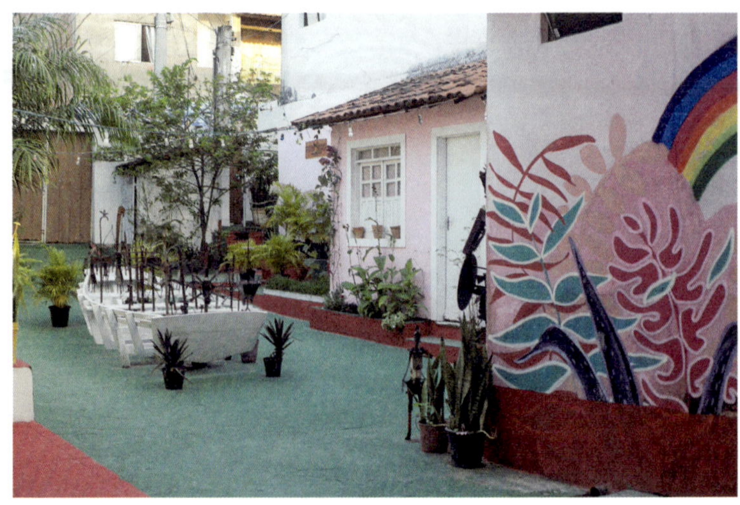

Instituto Oyá
Courtesy of the artist

waterfalls of Parque São Bartolomeu, a place with a remnant of Atlantic Forest. It's a beautiful place. This is where these children live. Every day they are at the Instituto and are welcomed by the educators on the fringes of these areas, who work together, teaching and learning, because with children you teach and learn at the same time.

They are children aged between ten and fourteen. Every day I have a group to work with. It's funny that one day I decided to work on Rubem Valentim's aesthetic. I put his work on the TV and they looked at it and said that's what they were going to do, and they started to develop a whole project. I was there watching and they were talking about what they understood and drawing. I told them I didn't want them to draw, I wanted them to think and cut out shapes for us to work with. Then one of them said: "but I need to draw, I need to show my drawing, so that later…" And he started giving me lessons. I thought: "I'm screwed." In other words, you don't have to say much, just put out good material and let the child have it, and they'll get a result. So that result can be a trigger.

That's what this place of education is all about. And it's a candomblé *terreiro*, where we don't mix. But they've mentioned Oxóssi, Xangô, I don't know what. Because it's a space that translates by itself, and then they start coming in, you find out that the grandmother has a *terreiro*, that the other grandmother goes to I don't know what, that the mother goes to such and such a place, that he likes such and such orixá, several come in here talking.

And we don't encourage anything, we just listen, understand and give care. The important thing is to care, to give attention. That's all children need to grow.

It's about working with language. What you've done is too modest, make it bigger. What you've done, make it grow. Next thing you know, he's done it. In other words, it's not the drawing itself, it's the growing up, when he cuts it larger, he empowers himself too. He understands that he can be bigger. So they're metaphors, they're ways of educating.

But we have to be the best. So it has to be the best for the people. The same material that I work with is the same material that I make available to them. There's no difference. The same, with everything. Everything I use, I give to them. And they look at it and start asking, asking, let them ask, they keep asking, you keep answering. And that is formative. When you leave here, you can't measure it, I always say that, but something will happen.

1   An African proverb of Ashanti origin, an ethnic group best known among the Akan peoples of Ghana, located in the western region of the African continent, which says that "It takes a whole village to raise a child."
2   Located in Salvador (BA), this territory boasts the title of the Blackest neighborhood outside the African continent, and whose Ilê Ayê Afro *bloco* is the main point of reference for local Black education and culture.
3   To find out more about the term, we recommend *De índio a negro, ou o reverso*, by Antônio Jorge Victor dos Santos Godi. Available at: periodicos. ufba.br/index.php/crh/article/view/18843/12213. Acessed in: 2024.
4   A traditional marketplace in Salvador, Bahia, known for popular and local commerce
5   Learn more about the history of the Afro blocos mentioned in this video series: Afros e Afoxés: A revolução do tambor. Available at: www.youtube. com/@salvadorcapitalafro9726/featured. Accessed in: 2025.
6   An afro *bloco* founded in 1979 by residents of the Itapuã neighborhood in Salvador.

Hadra... Hida... Hal

Maha Elmadi

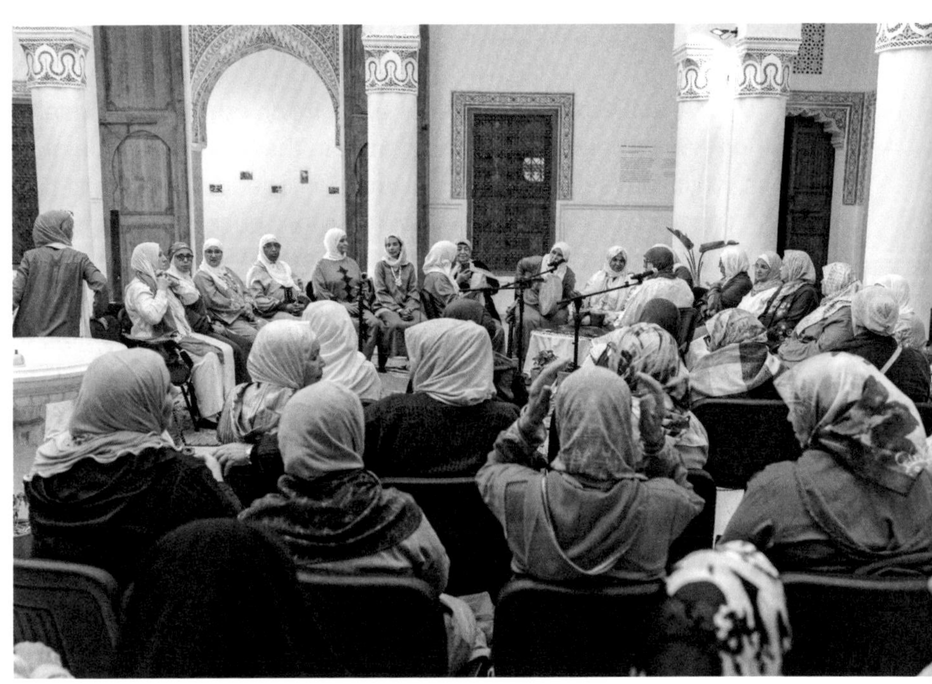

Lalla Khala,

Khalla...
Beauty spot.... The splendor of the soul... of the spirit
That grain of beauty that makes us human in our
                imperfection. l'Khalla,
My "maternal" aunt... this soulmate of the mother.

There is a Moroccan proverb that says
When your father dies, you still have your mother's heart
                to comfort your soul,
But if your mother disappears, you have only the doorway
                as a pillow.
But if you have an aunt, you will never be an orphan.

Khalla, l'khala, the heart and the aunt, this is the bond that
                holds us together and inspires me. Lalla Khala who gives
                without inheritance.
The mothers around you, in trance, unbound, free, carried
                by rhythm and voice, traveling through time, the times
                to come.
Hadra breaks the silence. My silence and the silence of the
                women hidden in time, on the sidelines. Today it's the
                voice that paves the way for tomorrow.

Laila, the night, the magic, the romance, the light of silence, this
                path of the neighborhood, an infinite back and forth
                between today and tomorrow, art, the image, the photo,
                the voice, the gaze, LE 18... space, Dar Bellarj,... the
                start...

Hadra... Hida... Hal... Trance. Moving on.

Like the Heartbeat

Anna Roberta Goetz

Everyone, everywhere and all the time, breathes.

Like the heartbeat, breathing connects all living creatures with each other.

It situates all of us in a moment in time, in simultaneity, with each other.

Like the heartbeat, breathing sets the rhythm of a life, the bassline.

It records the passing of time like a clock. One breath follows another.

Like the heartbeat, breathing is a continuous repetition of inhales and exhales:

Breathing in and out, again and again; sometimes faster, sometimes slower, shorter or longer.

An average of 23,000 breaths per day, 8.4 million breaths a year, and multiplied by x number of years, a lifetime.

At the *Invocation #1 – Souffles: On Deep Listening and Active Reception*, artist Simnikiwe Buhlungu spoke about the difference between looping and synthesis. Based on the premise that in looping the same fragment is repeated and that synthesis can thus be thought of as chronological looping, she asked whether a voice (even if it is optimized, an octave lower or equipped with a high-pass filter) from a historical moment would still be considered the same voice when heard in a future encounter.

Breathing is based on such a continuous repetition, a chronological looping. Every combined inhalation and exhalation, however, is interwoven with a moment in time and its circumstances, and is shaped by our physical, mental, and emotional state of being. So there is no breath like another.

Breathing situates us in a moment in time, and at the same time, every breath builds on the one that preceded it and lays ground for the one that follows.

By breathing, in and out, again and again, we establish a connection between moments in time and with each other in simultaneity.

There is only one first and last breath.

When a baby is born and brought into the world, their first cry marks their very first breath that causes the baby's lungs to expand and the circulatory system to adapt to life in this world. And the last breath, in its turn, marks the slow shutdown of the organic machinery that keeps us alive – consciousness fades and life in this world has come to an end.

In her welcoming note for the *Invocation* in Marrakech, my dear colleague Alya Sebti adapted Leo Asemota's question "when looking at the mirror, whom do you see?" to "looking at the mirror, what do you hear?" She therewith pointed out a horizontal and vertical connection in time and space that is established in the act of breathing – co-breathing so to speak – that connects us with all others who are in parallel breathing, as well as to those who were before us and those who are still to come breathing. No matter who, where and when we are – we all breathe. And in the act of breathing, we are all equal, theoretically. So, by breathing in silent togetherness and simultaneity, we affirm that equality, consciously or not.

In Marrakech, Bonaventure Soh Bejeng Ndikung invoked the spirit of the poet Rendra who, in his seminal poem "Sebuah Dunia Yang Marah" [An Angry World] (1960), repeated the question "How does the world breathe now?" over and over again to lament

> in utter awe the inscrutable state of the world today. The term "today" in its relativity and endless elasticity is that day, that week, that month, that moment in 1960 when the poem was written, and that point in time today, when you notice that the today of 1960 could easily step in as a surrogate for the today of now and vice versa.[1]

How is it possible that these moments of immense violence committed by people against other people are possible at all and then continue to repeat themselves? How are those who are in these moments still able to breathe? Maybe this breathing is an expression of holding on to the belief in humanity, that something can and will change? Does it perhaps reflect the belief in those who are still to come and who will do something different so those moments of enduring breathing will not be repeated?

Either way, focusing on conscious breathing in and out may well be the only way to breathe through these moments without losing your mind.

Unlike the heartbeat, breathing can be actively guided.

Although we breathe unconsciously most of the time, by controlling and regulating each inhalation and exhalation we have the power to change the way we feel in and with the very moment in time. Our breathing is therefore not only shaped by our physical, mental and emotional state – but is also capable of influencing it in turn. By conscious breathing, we can impact our body physically as much as psychologically, i.e. calm down our heart rate, lower your blood pressure, make pain feel different, or reduce our emotional stress level and cope with anxiety.

122 The conscious breathing is dependent on a *Deep listening* to one's own breathing – as the title of the *Invocation* in Marrakech promised.

In traditional Buddhist or Hindu practices, such as meditation and yoga, conscious breathing is utilized to gather the mental focus to the body and its movement in order to achieve a different state of mind completely present in the very moment. Also in Sufi's gatherings, like Hadras, such as those we were fortunate to experience in Marrakech as part of the first chapter of the 36th Bienal de São Paulo, performed by Les Mamans Douées, a group of women from the Dar Bellarj neighborhood that formed in 2008 after the death of Susanne Biedermann, the founder and spiritual mother of Dar Bellarj, on the initiative of Maha Elmadi, its director, to combat prejudices that reduce women to the role of mother or wife. The group has developed into a support system for those involved, in which they practice Sufi rituals or meet for workshops, theater plays or handicraft sessions.

In the central courtyard of Dar Bellarj, the women collectively and ostinato-like chanted religious poetic verses while synchronously bending forward, while exhaling, and straightening up again, while inhaling. The movement, together with the singing and breathing formed an overall hypnotic rhythm that mesmerized everyone present. This ritual went on for about two hours with several moments where the tension grew very high, for the contributing women as much as for the audience – everyone present supported the women's chanting by clapping and/or singing for most of the time. To witness this ritual – this listening to one another and breathing and moving in togetherness in collective presence, physically and emotionally, was a unique experience and an impactful reminder of how we are all connected with each other over time and space. Nothing exists outside. Breathing is being, being part of it.

1   See "How to Ventilate in an Airtight World" by Bonaventure Soh Bejeng Ndikung in this publication.

A Practice of Errantry

Omar Berrada

For and with
Christian Nyampeta

1.

how to live
how to gather
     untethered
to meander together
     through fields
         & forms of learning

we repair we
lend an ear
     to the earth
and shelter
        otherwise

2.

a haunting resolve
to undermine modernity
unhinge
           the stubborn repetition
of being-third
dissonate
           outside of all concept
write otherwise
the system will never define
           a fragment

we will study the silence
of utopia the corrosive irony
of realism the relentless judgment
of ruin the system
of our nerves
we will grasp at the seed

a digital database
of african expression
kampala & Kigali
maseru & mechelen
desediment the great lakes
see (y)our archive stutter
solidarity is presymbolic

3.

even their hand gestures were fascinating
even rest rusts as the result
                of a raised right fist
received in the public interiors of art
monasteries
        idiorrhythmy
every invariable liberation
                a whole locus of play
the implications of synchronicity
the pleasures of peace

her hair touched the grass
rhythms are invisible

4.

a quiet afternoon
a gated garden
the string the pebble
the pebble the string
an absence of adult fingers
order   sacrifice   distraction
controversial enforcement
the desert became an interior state

5.

what sound preceded my name
in the colonial sediments of capital
what if conversion
          is folklore
technology is divination
memory is interlude
how come the song – kwibuka –
how come the song's
digital deformities
          – tangible fade –
how shall we honor the victims
their monumental rhythms
of repose when new language
writes a new life
in the afterlife of nations

we live to regret
no one was nursed
by the rhythm of this cross
occupation is given
in a confluence of waters

6.

consider the prestige and presence
of portraiture a broad hat with feathers
what was the name of the congolese envoy
to receive a velvet coat a sash of gold
a ship was crossing the present order
of occasional translation's
speculative silver trimmings

reconsider the whole genealogy
of thought the censorship of muscle
insurgency   to philosophize
is to translate
                    – akan –
        a language of languages
putting logic
        to the test
of naïve reciprocity
a strange form of totality
genocidal humanism

7.

what is heard and what is danced
a different understanding
of sound the back and forth
the hum of felt
        the how of ear
the primary of organ
a music of images

indiscipline passes through
the stiff soliloquies of thought
a practice of errantry
in the encounter of self

rené descartes   zera yacob
un-
        spoken links
shape a grammar
of archival loss

philosophy reached a limit
in the scriptorium

8.

listen and presume
inhabit and refuse
an invitation to gather
a composition
         a form-of-law
that colonized the world
a quality of human
at the hands of the west
a practice of looking beyond
a capacity of being other
than a simple instrument

my critique of somnambulist
reason was a statement
         not a slander
call me mythologist
I give meaning
             to prefixes

        if I can wear another person
can I prevent the violence

only a few are free
to look after the heart
to ask about the trees
to live with the future

in the absence of outside
           we plant
interior sensibilities

An earlier version of these poems was published in Christian Nyampeta, *Togetherward*. Archive Books, 2022.

The poems borrow and recompose language from a set of texts assembled by Christian Nyampeta into a repository of reference materials for projects in progress. Of particular interest here were the following:
Bourahima Ouattara, "Fragmented Africa," translated by Christian Nyampeta, 2018; "Public Interior," Christian Nyampeta in conversation with Maaike Lauwaert, 2015; Armand Gauz, "The Dreams of Kong by Binger," translated by Christian Nyampeta, 2018; Souleymane Bachir Diagne, "Thinking from Language to Language," translated by Christian Nyampeta, 2018; Tina M. Campt, *Listening to Images*. Duke University Press, 2017; Séverine Kodjo-Grandvaux, "Mirror Effects: Thinking Africa, Thinking the World," translated by Christian Nyampeta, 2018; Denise Ferreira da Silva, "Togetherward," 2017; Maniragaba Balibutsa, "Les perspectives de la pensée philosophique Bantu-rwandaise après Alexis Kagame," translated by Christian Nyampeta 2019; Rose-Marie Mukarutabana, conversation with Isaïe Nzeyimana, in *A Communion of Spirits: Conversations in Arts and Philosophy*, filmed by Christian Nyampeta, 2018; Christian Nyampeta, "'In the Black Color of the Night': Theology and Philosophy in Exile," 2019.

The Power of Trance

Taoufiq Izeddiou

To me, a space of trance is first and foremost a space of freedom. It is in the here and now, renewed from one moment to the next, from one *Lila*[1] to the next. This means that the person entering the space of trance accepts to be carried away by this cosmogony, like the Gnawa, the Hmacha, or the Aissawa, for example.

I also see trance as a therapeutic space as well, because this experience depends on the person, on what they carry in their heart, on their energetic charge, and on what is happening in their social environment, in their life, and on how their body and soul resonate with everything that is happening in the world.

The space created in trance is therefore one of inspiration and creativity. It is also a space of freedom, because there is no protocol for entering a trance. It is the combination of our steps, our bodies, our ages, our wounds, our questions, and the twists and turns of life that we allow ourselves to take. I always say that when the mind is relaxed, the body is relaxed. That's why I think dances performed by women are more expressive, freer, and more spectacular, because most women, given the society we live in, carry a lot of heavy things and a lot of unspoken things. They often don't have much space to express themselves, to vent, to "get it all out." That's why these spaces are so important. I always say, while in the West you go to a psychiatrist, over here in Morocco we spend a night in a trance.

We come back to ourselves and we are taken care of by society. When I say that it is society that takes care of us, I don't mean in any way that we call the fire brigade or the ambulance when someone falls. That I mean is that it is we, as a society, that invents itself, after dancing to exhaustion.

This question of exhaustion is fundamental. How do you exhaust a system and how do you go from a political body to a poetic body? A political body that at first is fraught with tension is guided by its conquests. A tired body that loses its strength gives way to poetry. I think there is a fundamental truth in the moment of tiredness. In this transition from the political body to the poetic body many beautiful things emerge.

Fundamental to accessing this transition is the question of repetition. How does a movement, the same movement, or a leap or a repeated gesture, feed on time and space? How can we not relax so that it too becomes another, even if we are still in the same movement? How does this movement evolve and, therefore, how does our body, in its fatigue, manage to produce dance, gesture, energy, and movement? It's at this precise moment that we mustn't relax or exhaust ourselves. Because the exact moment when we become tired it all begins. A performer who takes on that strength, that anger, and that trance energy is a

135

performer who can communicate this transition, because their movement is not vain. It is full of emotions, energy, and the intangible. That's the power of dance. We have to dig into the dark holes of our being for those things we dare not face. We must go there in search of the source of inspiration and perseverance, in search of continuity and creativity.

The Lila Gnawa trance is characterized by seven colors. Each of these seven colors illustrates a part of our personality. Yellow, for example, expresses the feminine side, green expresses our spirituality, and blue expresses the spirits above our heads, the sea and the sky. I'm very interested in red because in the Gnawa culture one associated red with sound. All over the world, we are with sound. Both with sound and with love, and this meeting of the two is very important. That's why I use red and black a lot in my dramaturgy, to talk about the question of the unknown, the mystery that the color black carries and its encounter with the power of sound.

We find trance all over the world: there's voodoo in Haiti, zar in Egypt, whirling dervishes in Turkey, butoh in Japan or even techno music. All these sources are reflected in my work.

But it is from the Gnawa or Hmadja trance tradition that I nourish the form that is questioned in this performance. I have used trance as a source of pedagogy and learning for today's contemporary dancer, who relies on steps, rhythms, freedom of expression, the question of resistance and what the guembri is capable of unlocking. The sound of this ancestral instrument is not trivial. Composed of cashew wood and goat intestines turned inside out to form the double bass, it touches on something visceral. And when you play, the sound goes straight to the heart, to the depths of the soul. It goes beyond and frees itself from the territory of the brain to take over the body and heart. This is what causes many things to evolve in Gnawa. And this is the power of trance as a space to evolve as human beings.

137

Can You Feel It

Conversation with Simnikiwe Buhlungu and Thiago de Paula Souza

Thiago de Paula Souza: Sound has always been a significant element in your art practice. When we invited you to participate in the first *Invocation*, you mentioned your interest in the Gnawa tradition. What exactly were you researching?

Simnikiwe Buhlungu: I had been familiar with Gnawa as a *listener of it as music* rather than a researcher of a particular history. I hadn't dived into the depths that I later accessed. I think it is important to include and make space for the practice of listening to music and hold off on treating it as an immediate portal to "research."

> **TdPS:** I agree. But one cannot deny that listening could be an entry to a larger subject of research, sometimes it can work as a means to start to think and learn about different contexts. I'm curious to understand more if and how listening appears as an artistic tool for you.

SB: I will start with a kind of anecdote. When I think of *listening*, I think of it as something that, growing up, *to listen* was something you needed to do. And that there was an importance to that act, to that verb. And listening, as an example, listening to something an elder would say, listening to a proverb, listening to the intonation of how something is said, is really important as a kind of transgenerational key. So listening, in a way, was not like this optional thing. It was really like, you need to pay attention, you really need to listen. And you kind of knew, like, even if there were moments of wanting to rebel or push against that, to put it simply, there's a reward that comes after that discipline, or that kind of sustained attention, or a sustained relationship with this act. I mean, when you're a kid, you kind of want to do millions of things, right? But when an elder is speaking to you, I think for many kinds of contexts and cultures, it becomes very forma-tive in how you understand this thing. And then, of course, the elements of, oh, you weren't listening, or you didn't listen. Why weren't you listening?

Which can be punitive, but I understand the act of listening as something quite crucial because it's saying something, right? So when taking this idea or this relationship to listening as a practice within my practice, but also as elemental and artistic research, for me it's really that kind of, it's not just like listening for fun, but there's something that is unlocked by sustaining that relationship. And that thing that's unlocked doesn't necessarily have to be an answer, but can be more questions. So, for example, with Gnawa, you asked, what's your relationship to it? And I was like, I only know it as music I would listen to, you know, not that I delved into the history. But I do think coming to Marrakech, as an example of listening through and sustaining that relationship of listening to Gnawa music within that context and hearing what everybody else is sharing, that's when it kind of unlocked, like, oh, wait, this is actually what this is about. This is what this history is about. This is what this context is about. So I think just to also illustrate, for me, listening as a way of building research is also about that sustained kind of sitting with the verb, right, to sit alongside the verb, not to just do it. And then also to sit with the fact that maybe it takes a very long time to realize what you're listening for. Listening, I also like to think of it in terms of synthesis, you know like electronic signals, the fact that when you're listening to a song, you think of it as a song, but you're listening to mathematics, you're listening to physics.

> **TdPS:** We're listening to wiggles and sine waves. That's what you're listening to. So how to sustain through that to kind of understand what the sound is saying afterwards?

SB: I think that what also helped expand my artistic process of researching was just to sit with those moments of, like, okay, what is actually happening here, rather than just being, like, oh, this is an acid house song from the 1980s. Yes, it is, but also you're listening to physics.

> **TdPS:** Your presentation started in a very nuanced way: you proposed this kind of entanglement, between synthesis, intonation, looping, listening, and active reception. These five elements seem to belong to the same world, yet each has its own role.

SB: So, I was actually speaking to someone about this anecdote earlier, that someone in London many years ago told me about growing up in a multichannel installation, and I'm like, what does that mean? And they said, I grew up in a house where in one room the radio was on, in another room the TV was on, another room there's someone shouting, another room it's the sound of the oven or the kitchen, and the washing machine, and that in listening to something specific, there's something else going on, whether it's next to you, whether it's outside, whether it's in the next room. If you're in a cave and you think you're only hearing yourself and the sound of your voice echoing, there's something else going on.

So, this kind of reminds me of the plurality and polyphony in listening, and that it's not like this isolated singular kind of thing

140

that's going on. Thinking of, I don't know, an elder telling me a story, the sound of a car in the background, the sound of someone else calling them, the sound of an interruption, a pause, the sound of forgetting where you were in the story and having to think, oh, where was I again? The sound of a cell phone ringing. These elements of sound and sounding are really important because we cannot… I don't think it's useful to think of listening as an isolated practice. It's one that has to be negotiated in terms of the thing that you are listening to and that balancing act of all those things we have to listen to.

> **TdPS:** During your presentation, you invited us to listen closely to "Can You Feel It," by Larry Heard/Mr. Fingers. Could you share more about your connection to that song? If I understand correctly, do you feel a particular resonance with it?

SB: You might not believe me, but I know this song because of a video game. So, to set the scene: It's 2005, and there's a new video game that's come out for PlayStation 2, and it's called *Grand Theft Auto: San Andreas*. And in this game, you can drive cars, and they have different radio stations. The game is based on a fictional iteration of somewhere in the United States. One of the radio stations only plays house music, and "Can You Feel It" would play repeatedly, and there was something about this bass, this kind of wobbly but very tight bass. But then also becoming older, really digging into, like, what is actually the history behind this classic house music? Then, you know, you start learning about Detroit house music, but then there's also Chicago, so there's a bit of beef there. And learning about a song like "Can You Feel It" and the context it came from. Music can teach us about a moment, like a context, even if we are not directly connected to it.

> **TdPS:** Right. So, a song you first heard as a child became the key that allowed you to understand a context that is distant not only geographically but also socially?

SB: Exactly. I realized that this song wasn't just the background music to a video game I encountered at age ten – it was actually the soundtrack to a specific sociopolitical context in the 1980s, a time before I was even born. That understanding led me to dive deeper into what was happening during that period. So "Can You Feel It" isn't just an incredible club track. People were playing it as a means of safety, resistance, protest, and release. And then from that history, learning about, okay, who's

141

Mr. Fingers/Larry Heard? Who are these people? How were they making house music at the time using an entry-level kind of instrument? Maybe one person has a synth, and then all of them come to that one person's house to make something. So it's not just, again, about the song itself, but the context in which the song is operating and how that slowly reveals itself.

TdPS: And when was the moment when you, as an adult, realized there was another use for the track?

SB: I started getting into the synth world, not as a synth nerd, but just genuinely fascinated by the use of electricity to do so many interesting things within Black cultural production, then learning that the bassline of the song was made by a synth, which I have, which is the Juno-6. It's a synthesizer made by Roland, and Roland is a Japanese company. So, just in terms of the song, which comes from Chicago in the United States, it reached me in South Africa. Okay, so the song from the 1980s in the United States came to me in South Africa in 2005, and was made with a synthesizer, also from the 1980s, from Japan. You have, like, a geographical kind of movement happening here because of the song and because of this bassline, and it's really an unforgettable bassline. This is also seen as the song that kind of opens up. It's like Sunday school. It's an educational program as a song.

TdPS: You often talk about the elders, and one moment that stood out in your presentation was when you discussed the transgenerational loop. I want to understand what a loop means to you. I know it's not just repetition in your view, but how do you define it, not just in terms of sound or music, but more broadly?

SB: I think of it as not only repetition, because I think repetition implies it feels very linear and strict and boxy and just like the same of the same of the same. I mean, I would like to think of repetition or looping as a Fibonacci sequence with leaves that repeat themselves but change scale or positional sequentially. They're not exactly the same, you know what I mean?

TdPS: Yeah, what they call repetitive construction, similar to fractals.

142

SB: So for me, looping is really the extension of something. Looping is a library. It's also not this idea of a perfect circle, but something that, with each revolution, with each turn, picks up something and drops something else, and picks something else, like a wheel, right? Picking up dirt and dropping water, like really this kind of picking up, but there's an accruing of knowledge or accruing of something with each revolution. And also the loss of something, of some things through time. Things don't stay exactly the same. So there's also space for deviation within.

 TdPS: Yes, and even with all these rotations, something always remains.

SB: I like to think of the loop as a library with deviation in some capacity, but also the ability to hold, right? The ability to store. And in that way, because even though it deviates, it's still quite a reliable kind of methodology of knowledge.

 TdPS: When we were in Marrakech we met Maalem Abdellah El Gourd, and we learned that he had performed with Randy Watson, who moved to Morocco and spent, like, years and years of his life researching music in the African continent.

SB: It was during this period that he recorded *Blue Moses*, right?

 TdPS: Yeah, deeply inspired by Gnawa. I was just thinking here now in a certain sense, it feels that he was trying to re-establish the loop, when I thought about your notion of loop, your notion of the transgenerational loop. Do you think your encounter with "Can You Feel It" represents a kind of transgenerational loop? In a way, you're re-establishing, or even mending a lost connection. Music, in this sense, can serve as a mending element – but it doesn't necessarily have to be music. Any form of artistic practice can function as a means to mend something or to establish a new loop.

SB: Yeah, for the sharing in Marrakech, yes, but just, like, sitting with that sound for many years, no. I don't think I was able to articulate what I was doing, what the fascination with the song was. I mean, more so because I've never heard that song in a club, and I've never danced to that song. It's also this kind of, like, I've heard that song on TV speakers, and headphones, and laptop speakers, and maybe a Bluetooth speaker. So the transmission is also part of this, of how it's facilitating, and how... and also then it leaves a gap of, like, I'm waiting, or maybe I'm curious about when the encounter will be, when I do hear it in a club.

And maybe that would also be this kind of metaphorical mending of this loop, which is really to hear it in its context, its intended context. That's also really exciting, because there are obviously many different points in which you can come to the song, and the history of the song, but there's also something really special with listening to it in that kind of place that it sits in historically. So for me also, I've been sitting alongside the song, now I say twenty years, but I can imagine sitting with it another twenty years, and hopefully in that next twenty years I hear it in a club, or maybe I hear it through my phone again, right?

TdPS: Perhaps you've heard a sample of the song in a club and haven't really realized it.

SB: Yeah, that's also the subtlety of sampling, it's also an extension of looping, but like a piece of, I mean, sampling is literally DNA, that's like DNA going on, right? There's biology happening with this ability for a body to kind of embed itself in something else, silently, quietly, for whatever reason, or maybe quite loudly and overtly. Sampling is also really interesting in that it is constantly a negotiation in terms of who was sampling, what they were sampling, how they were sampling, what laws they were trying to evade by sampling.

TdPS: How do those three elements – sampling, synthesis, and looping – come together? How can they serve as a passageway, allowing sound to transcend into another realm? That's essentially what you aim to do, right? You never abandon the sonic world. But rather, you use these elements to travel, to move sound into a broader context, expanding its reach beyond its original form.

SB: I like to think of sampling as a tool anyway in my practice, even with things that are not sound, like materially sampling. But it's also, maybe also another cheesy thing to say, but to evade capture, to continue. But then sampling also as a way of embedding other contexts and histories within all of that. I kind of see the three of them working together as a way of structuring the way in which a story is told, or structuring a way in which knowledge is disseminated, and using them deliberately as tools outside of the sonic world, and I think that's also some of the beauty of sound as a space in terms of a language. And maybe it's easier to access as a visual artist because I'm not a musician, so I think I also have the privilege and the leeway to start to think about these different methodologies outside of them as music production tools, but I'm really thinking about them in a completely different context that allows for us to arrive at the ocular at a later stage.

Silence

Ghassan El Hakim

Have you already tried to catch the silence, put it into a bottle, and close the bottle? Will the silence stay alone in the bottle, or will it mix with another substance inside? Maybe that is why, when you place your ear near the bottle, you can hear the sound of the sea: wouldn't that be the mixture of the silence and the substance in the bottle?

When we are near a place with a lot of people, with noise, hubbub and din, can we open the bottle and throw the silence at them?

Or, when a friend of ours keeps complaining and asking the same questions, can we present him with a bottle of silence?

Since my childhood, I've been looking for my paternal grandfather… On my mother's side, everything is white, clear, scripted, recorded: we even have a family tree that goes back to the Prophet! On my father's side everything is black, dark, ambiguous, nothing is said, nothing is scripted… In my father's family my questions have always met silent replies: where was my grandfather from? Silence… Did he really walk from Tata to Fes? Silence… I was told he died as he was leaving the mosque! Silence… And what is his family name, his tribe, his origin in one word? Silence, or a fabricated narrative: I'd rather have silence than that fabricated story.

That silence created a void in my mind, which I could fill with anything or nothing.

By the way I myself became a silent person… I sometimes have answers to questions that are put to me, but I keep silent, as though the absolute silence above my head, which I had to bear for all my childhood and adolescence, should keep ruling up there… Then I left to study in Paris and I forgot about all those stories, then I came back to Morocco and decided to settle in Casablanca…

One night I called my father to check on him, and at the end of our chat, I don't know why, I asked him: "How old were you when your father died?" – "Thirteen." – "And he?" – "Eighty-six!"… – "Eighty-six: you mean you were born to him when he was seventy-three! Wait, wait, if my calculation is right, my father was born in 1955. If I subtract 73, i.e. my grandfather's age when my father was born, I get my grandfather's birth date: 1955 minus 73 equals 1882!" Silence, on my part this time. A frozen silence that caught my nape, then spread like a panic attack: my arm started tingling, my mouth went dry, palpitation in my heart, all that would roll down my belly like a ball: I could no longer control that silence, which scared me, then it turned into a deep blues like a tear pent up for a hundred years, since that 19th century. Then I started heeding voices, shouts, horses galloping, I could see *caïds* chase *rouguis*, rebels, and cut off their heads, whose hair was combed in a horn-shaped braid, I could see the 19th century passing before me, and I pictured that other Morocco, that other time, that other way of life, that other way of breathing, of eating, of sitting, of walking, of considering the world… Even the word "other" is a deep silence in the history of modern Morocco!

I found myself trapped between two silences: my family's little silence, and my country's deep silence. Then I decided to walk and, as my friend Mbarek says, as you walk, you think with your feet! I wanted to walk over the distance my grandfather had covered a hundred years before me. I wanted to walk all the way from Fes to Tata, 800 kilometers! I started with a stepover in the High Atlas, between Demnate and Ouarzazate, a 100-kilometer walk that I covered in six days. Then I returned to Casablanca, filled with the silence of a mountain, but in the midst of that silence, I seemed to hear the name of my grandfather's village – "Adis," which means "belly" in the Tamazight language!

When I came back I called my father to give him the good news: "I found the name of your father's village." – "Who told you?" – "Didn't you whisper it to me before I started my journey?" – "No, I don't know that name." I called my mother and she gave me the same answer. I called my cousin Fatiha, who lives in France and helps me in my quest for that lost origin: same answer, she didn't know that name! Then I called all the members of my father's family who I knew, and even those I didn't know, and they all told me they knew nothing about that name!

I became obsessed by the silence of my dead grandfather, and of my father!

I couldn't bear that any longer, so I decided to tear down my father's wall of silence with a provocation; I called him one evening and said to him: "You know, your father died without leaving a family name to you, he didn't even register your birth at the registry office, he didn't even leave you with a story which you could tell your children, some kind of a personal legend! Moreover, your mother Hania, my grandmother, may God bless her soul, do you know how old she was when you were born to her? She was twenty, and your father was seventy-three, he was fifty-three years older than her, doesn't this mean anything to you? Don't you read this as a sign? Don't you think she was given to him as a present? And her name is Hania, which means the meek, and her sister's name, Fadila, means the virtuous, her brother Mbarek's name means the blessed, and their father's name is Tayeb, the good one: all these names are slaves' names, mate!"

A twofold silence: my own, and my father's! After that, I stopped talking to him about all that. And the birth of my daughter Mina

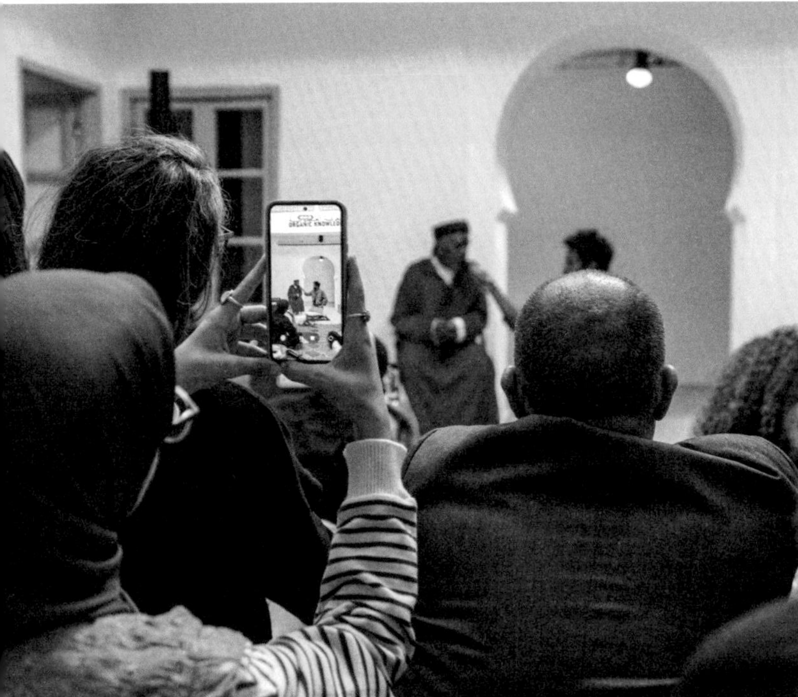

helped me do that. And I joined my father's silence, or my mother's, or both… A family silence, an inherited silence! A silence we leave as a legacy to our children!

Four years later I was in Amsterdam, where I met a theater group called Female Economy, who offered me to participate in a theater residence in Tangier, that revolves around an adoption concept. And on top of all that, the director, a lady as mad as a hatter called Adelheid Roosen, chose for me, as the place for my adoption, the home of Gnawa in Tangier, which is the most discreet, secret, mysterious music ever. And who else with, but the Gnawa master Abdellah El Gourd, the most calm, silent master, the Buddha of Gnawa in Morocco?! On the first day of adoption we didn't talk, the next day we exchanged a few words, and on the third day I started to understand: I understood that the Maalam's silence wasn't a mere silence. His silence is filled, with words, music, gestures, messages, subversion, things untold, and I said to myself maybe my grandfather's, father's and the Maalam's silences were a kind of *muqawama*, a kind of protest, of insubordination, of insurrection, a kind of resistance against what I call voluntary amnesia.

149

The author thanks Jean Albert
Margaine for the translation
from French.

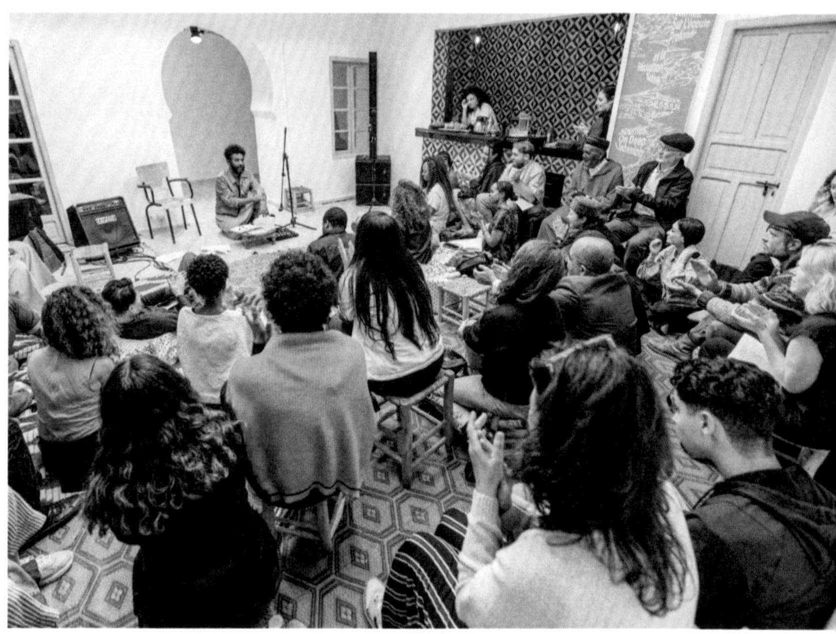

150

Grandpa,

My mother's name is Rajae, which means "hope" in Arabic, and she does give hope to all the people who come across her! My mother comes from a great family, a royal family who fled from the slaughter of the Abbassi dynasty in Baghdad, centuries ago, and had left everything behind except hope! It was my mother who first talked to me about you! Indeed you never met, but she knows you through my father: Unlike him, she mentioned your existence and raised a hope deep down in me, a quest I had to achieve: to find you. My mother is very different from the other members of her family, and I came into existence thanks to that difference. They always denied her the right to marry my father, but she persevered and followed her heart: we're like that in our family, like my mother. We never give up. My father, your son, is not like my mother, he gives up easily, he never follows his ideas till the end, never follows his heart. But I am like my mother. If one day you come to see us, you'll be happy to meet my mother. She no longer lives with my father, their love story did not end well. It began in Amsterdam, in the Vondelpark... But my mother still values their beautiful story. She has no hard feelings. My father went through hard times after you left, and only my mother was able to manage the frustration of that story and of being rejected. Sometimes I say to myself that if you had not been gone, my parents would have never met, so I think your departure was a good thing in the end and it allowed me to come into existence. My mother told me you were a pious, God-loving man, who prayed a lot, but unfortunately we are not like that at all in my family: my mother taught me to love, not to pray... My mother is very sensitive, so much so that she faints when she hears any music. I think I realized that when I was a kid living alone with my mother in Asilah, in northern Morocco. We were in the sitting room of our little house with a well, when all of a sudden my mother started dancing, and twirling, shaking her head, her hair covering her eyes. That was caused by music coming from outside, soaring up to our sitting room in our little house with the well. My aunt had come for a visit, we looked out of the window to see which musicians made my mother move in that manner, and my aunt whispered to my ear: "they are Gnawa musicians," then she slammed the window shut, as if she wanted to prevent the haunting music to get in and reach my mother's ears. At that precise moment I heard a scream, and when I turned back my mother had fainted! Do you know about the Gnawa, grandpa? Do you also fall down when you hear them?

151   I love you grandpa, even though I never met you!

Who is Ahmed Ben Draoui?

Laila Hida

In post-colonial Morocco of the 1960s, as the country recovered from its struggle for independence, a new Arab-Muslim national identity emerged as the unifying standard around which all sections of society were expected to rally. The cultural groups that were once dominant before colonization, now reduced to minorities, were forced to assimilate into this new model, influenced by both the promise of pan-Arabism and the allure of the modern West.

On this path, the destinies of many young people and families collided with profound change. They left their ancestral lands to seek opportunities in urban centers, turning their backs on age-old traditions, now seen as archaic and primitive by the new dominant culture. Over three generations, layers of unspoken stories, traumas, cultural and class assimilations, broken dreams, repressed desires, struggles for emancipation, longings for return, ruptures, and misunderstandings accumulated, giving rise to complex, fragmented identities. These identities, like fractured memories, return in fleeting glimpses to haunt each character in the unfolding narrative.

The following text reveals three snapshots from different eras. It is read as one observes an image, and like any image, it shows only the visible part of the story. What unfolds in the silences is precisely the space between reality and imagination where history is forged.

The text was read by Laila Hida at the *Invocation*, accompanied by multi-instrumentalist musician Mourad Belouadi with his electro-acoustic machine and guembri.

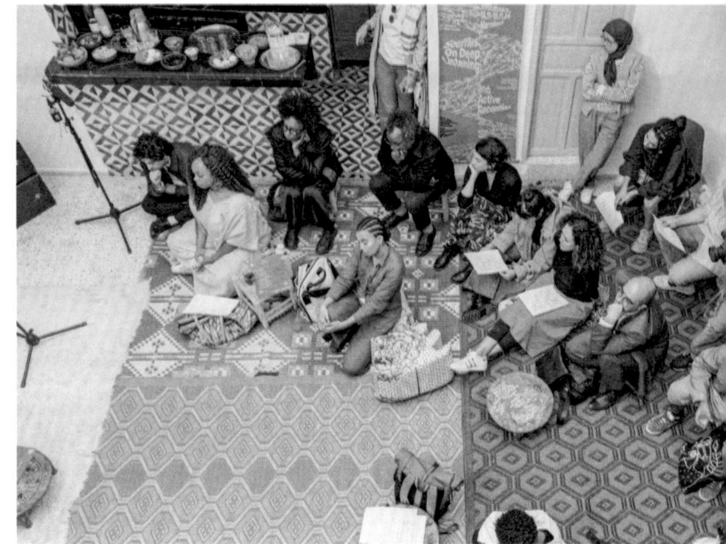

Act I

Exile

Ahmed Ben Draoui was born in 1915, in the Oasis of Figuig,
just meters from the Algerian border.

In his village, the name Draoui [black] was rare.
No other families bore it,
maybe his father, El Mekki Draoui, came from elsewhere,
or maybe it was tied to the color of his skin.

Ahmed died; his story untold.

In 1960, Abdelaziz, one of Ahmed's sons,
just sixteen, left the oasis for Casablanca.
Like so many of his generation, chasing dreams in the city.

But independence came with its own fractures:
the family broke under the weight of disputes,
inheritance battles,
gardens abandoned,
the *Ksour* left empty.

Exile swept the children away.
    Figuig, like so many places, saw an exodus in those post-
                independence years.

Casablanca, 1965

Abdelaziz wanders downtown Casablanca,
and there's Abdellatif, his cousin, his friend.
They shared the law school benches since arriving in the city.

They grab coffee at La Chope,
their usual spot in Prince Moulay Abdellah.
Later, they're joined by Mustapha and L'Houssin.
Talk about protests, about student demonstrations,
change feels close.

But as night falls, Mustapha invites them home.
His mother, a *m'qadma* [priestess], is preparing a Lila –
          a night of trance.
Healing for Lalla Rkia,
haunted since her husband left for France.

Piled into a cab,
the chaos of Casablanca blurs into their thoughts.
Carrières Centrales welcomes them –
Crowded hub for the working class
Mustapha's family's home,
benefit from his father's railway work.

February cold forces them inside.
The Lila has begun.
The *Koyo* play *Wlad Bambra*.
The boys settle opposite the *Maalem* [master] and his musicians.

Lalla Mina's house hums with the spirit world.

It will be a long night.

Dance.
Trance.
Trance.
Dance.
Pieces of creation unravel till dawn.

Sla'a'nbi
Wlud Bambara
Nuqcha
Ada
Bouhala
Mimouna
Al Musawiyin
Al'homer
Esh-shorfa
Ulad El ghaba
Lalla Aicha
L-Yalat

Sweat.
Tears.
Exhaustion.
The body falls.
Spirits are satisfied.

The *guembri* slows,
the *qraqeb* fall silent.
Abdelaziz is on the ground,
his first trance.

Day breaks.
The guests stir as if waking from a dream.
Bowls of *Hssoua* – barley soup – revive them.

A month later, a student revolt erupts,
violently crushed.

Abdelaziz leaves the university for marriage.
A new life begins with Khadija, his cousin.
But the idealism dies.

He lives a quiet, settled life.
Yet, in the shadows,
he returns to the *Lilas*.

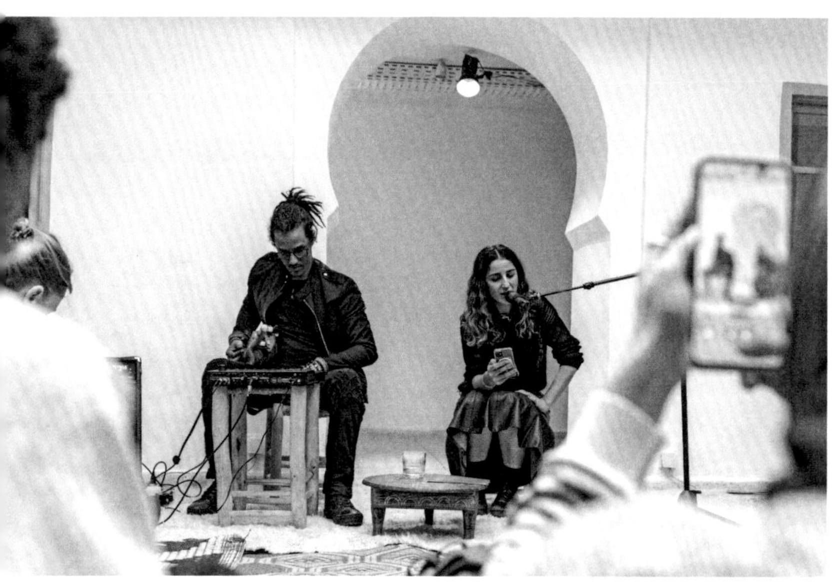

Trance becomes his refuge,
his escape from the alienation,
from the buried dreams,
the pain he can't speak of.

Act II

The Photograph

In a black-and-white photo from 1920,
five Black musicians stand in line,
draped in white tunics, black belts tied tight,
adorned with cowrie shells –
currency of the past, symbols of wealth and trade.

The man in the middle grips a Ganga drum,
goatskin stretched, painted with patterns,
geometric lines and dots.
(Nganga – it means healer in Bantu lands).
Beside him, four others hold Qraqeb –
metal castanets, sharp and rhythmic.

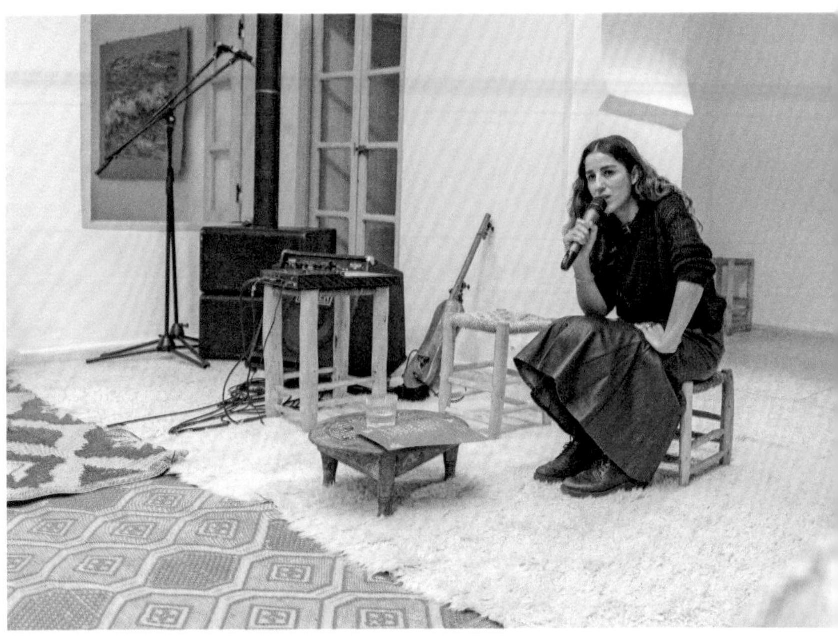

In the upper right-hand corner, the photo speaks:
Casablanca – Les Guinaguas [Indigenous musicians],
a 5-centime stamp, a postmark pressed.
The backdrop? Fake. The figures? Unreal.
They look like a painting, frozen in time.

An American scholar draws a line –
colonial cameras capturing, categorizing,
creating myths of Gnawa,
street performers becoming identities.

Here, the gap widens:
secret rituals, kept for the few,
and public rhythms,
pushed into "world music."

Look closer at this photograph.
It could've been taken today, almost unchanged.
The representation fixed in place,
while everything else moves, shifts, evolves.

For decades, scholars searched the Gnawa,
seeking meaning, finding the unknown.
The Gnawa world consumes those who ask,
leading them to confront their own *Mlouks* [spirits].

Photography tries to hold the visible,
erase the silence,
fix the fleeting.
But it distorts, it imprisons,
repeating the violence of domination.

Trance –
Trance breaks the frame.
Trance frees the Gnawa from the photograph.

Act III

L'Ghoul [The Ogre]

My name is Walid, grandson of Ahmed Ben Draoui.
This is a memory from my childhood, tangled with a memory
            from my mother's.

In her story, my mother walks down a dark alley in Figuig oasis,
in eastern Morocco, with her little brother Slimane – my uncle.
It was the 60s.

As they made their way toward Jnane Zitoun, the family garden,
they turned a corner in the narrow alleys of Ksar Znaga.
And there, they froze.

Face to face with a giant.
A giant and his camel.

The man, tall beyond belief, said in Arabic –
            a foreign tongue to them –
"*Heidou men triq*" – get out of the way.

Terrified, they ran home, their little bodies trembling,
shaking as they told their mother they'd seen a *Djinn*.
A towering figure, impossibly tall,
with a camel, speaking in a strange language.

A Figuig man couldn't be that tall.
And there were no camels in Figuig.

What they didn't know then was that their world,
the fortified Ksour surrounded by gardens,
was not so isolated.

Beyond the vast palm grove lay nomadic Arab families,
camel herders and traders,
wandering through.

Figuig, an Amazigh enclave,
had stayed self-sufficient for so long,
its people rarely imagined life beyond their oasis.
Strangers weren't just unfamiliar – they carried a sense of
            mystery, as if they belonged to another realm entirely.

My mother and Slimane kept telling this story as we grew up,
like a warning,
teaching us about the spirits,
the unseen forces that walk beside us.

Fast-forward to the late 80s,
to Hay Chmaou, a working-class neighborhood in Salé.
I was playing soccer in the street with my cousins,
outside my grandparents' house.

And from a distance,
we saw him.

A tall, Black man walking toward us,
slow, with enormous strides,
beating the *Ganga.*

As he got closer, he grew taller,
and taller.

He wore a black velvet headdress,
topped with a pompom spinning as he moved.
Small white cowrie shells glistened against the dark fabric.

The drumbeat thudded through the ground,
vibrating beneath our feet.
Terrified, we ran.
Straight home, shouting to my grandmother –
"L'Ghoul! L'Ghoul!" [The ogre]

She smiled, calming us in Tamazight,
a language I didn't understand.

She told us this man was a Gnawi,
a wandering healer,
a bringer of *Baraka* [good fortune].

This Gnawi would often knock on my grandparents' door,
seeking alms and spreading blessings.

Since the day my father fell into a trance,
my grandmother always kept a hot meal ready,
for pilgrims, healing musicians,
and those who carried the *Baraka.*

About the Authors

Alberto Pitta works with textile printing and screen printing, as well as painting and sculpture. He created prints featured in Afro-Brazilian Carnival groups such as Olodum, Filhos de Gandhy, and Cortejo Afro, which he founded. His works incorporate symbols, shapes, and patterns that evoke traditional African and Afro-diasporic elements, particularly those rooted in Yoruba mythology.

Alya Sebti is a curator and director of the ifa-Galerie (Institut für Auslandsbeziehungen) in Berlin, where she initiated the research and exhibition platform *Untie to Tie – On Colonial Legacies in Contemporary Societies*. She was co-curator of the Manifesta in Marseille (2020), guest curator of the Dakar Biennale (2018), and artistic director of the Marrakech Biennale (2014). She has led curatorial research through mentorship programs at the ZK/U artist residency (Berlin) and at MACAAL (Marrakech).

Amina Agueznay is a multidisciplinary artist who combines elements of structure, reinterpreted traditional mediums, and collective participation in pieces that vary in scale. Her monumental installation artworks are often based on collaborative projects, in an ongoing dialogue with artisans. Combining architectural and archaeological structure with the

163

work of the hand, her body of work evokes the transmission.

Anna Roberta Goetz is a curator and writer. She has worked at the Marta Herford Museum and the MMK Museum für Moderne Kunst Frankfurt. She was assistant curator and project manager of the German Pavilion at the 55th Venice Biennale (2013). She has organized major solo and group exhibitions in various countries and has taught at several international art academies, including the Zurich University of the Arts and the Städelschule in Frankfurt. Her publications include *Rodney McMillian: The Land: Not Without a Politic*, co-edited with Kathleen Rahn (2024), and *Cinthia Marcelle – By Means of Doubt*, co-edited with Isabella Rjeille (2023).

Bonaventure Soh Bejeng Ndikung is a curator, author, and biotechnologist, currently serving as the director and chief curator of the Haus der Kulturen der Welt (HKW) in Berlin. He is the founder and former artistic director of SAVVY Contemporary (Berlin), as well as the artistic director of sonsbeek20→24, a quadrennial contemporary art exhibition in Arnhem. He is a professor and head of faculty in the Master's program in Spatial Strategies at the weißensee academy of art berlin. His published works include, among others, *The Delusions of Care* (2021), *An*

Ongoing-Offcoming Tale: Ruminations on Art, Culture, Politics and Us/Others (2022), and *Pidginization as Curatorial Method* (2023).

Fatima-Zahra Lakrissa is an independent curator and researcher. She is interested in the layered subjectivities of European modern art history and the construction of Moroccan modernism through the works of artists engaging with the vernacular. Her research is oriented towards the sociology and history of the artistic avant-garde in Morocco during the 1960s and 1970s.

Ghassan El Hakim is an actor, director, and cultural programmer. He graduated from the Institut supérieur d'Art dramatique et d'Animation culturelle (ISADAC) in Rabat (2007) and completed an internship at the Conservatoire National Supérieur d'Art Dramatique (Paris). Awarded at the Yallah Film Festival in 2011, he stood out as both an actor and creator. In 2015, he became the programmer of the cultural center l'uZine, and currently, he directs and teaches at the art school La Parallèle in Casablanca, both in Casablanca.

Kenza Sefrioui is a cultural journalist, literary critic, and publisher. She was in charge of the literary section of the journal *Hebdomadaire*. She wrote the doctoral thesis in comparative literature at the Université Paris-Sorbonne *Souffles (1966-1973), espoirs de révolution culturelle au Maroc* (2013).

Keyna Eleison is a curator, researcher, and educator in art and culture. She coordinated all public institutions from the Rio de Janeiro Municipal Department of Culture and taught at the Escola de Artes Visuais do Parque Lage, where she was also a teaching coordinator. She was the curator of the 10th Bienal Internacional de SIART (2018), in Conchabamba, and 1st Bienal das Amazônias (2023), the artistic director of the MAM Rio (2020-2023) and director of research and content at the Bienal das Amazônias.

Laila Hida is an artist. She founded LE 18 in 2013. Hida's work uses private spaces and narratives to explore the place of the individual within a society gripped by change. She investigates projections and frictions of desire, imaginaries, and fantasies in both local and Western contexts through curation, publishing, installations, and photography projects.

Leila Bencharnia is a sound artist, acousmatic interpreter, and musician. Her sonic work is composed of analogic material including tapes, vinyls, and synthesizers.

Maha Elmadi has been the director of the Dar Bellarj Foundation in Marrakech since 2007. She is the initiator of the Mamans douées group and concept, and also created the Achoura festival.

Mirella Maria has a bachelor's degree in visual arts from Universidade Estadual Júlio de Mesquita Filho (Unesp). She holds a master's degree in visual arts and education from the same institution. Creator of the artistic project Quilombo Mulheres Negras, with seminars, exhibitions, and artistic experiences produced by Black women. She works with photography, collages, and textile art are permeated, bringing symbolic resignifications in the field of plasticity, memory, and existence.

Miriam Alves is a writer, social worker, and teacher. She made her literary debut in 1982 in the anthology *Axé: Antologia Contemporânea de Poesia Negra Brasileira* and in *Cadernos Negros* 5, a publication organized by the historic collective Quilombhoje. She published two poetry books: *Momentos de busca* (1983) and *Estrelas no dedo* (1985). She is also the author of the novels *Bará na trilha do vento* (2015) and *Mareia* (2019), the short story collections *Mulher mat(r)iz* (2011) and *Juntar pedaços* (2021), as well as the essay "BrasilAfro autorrevelado" (2010). Along with Arnaldo

Xavier and Cuti, she wrote the dramatic text *Terramara* (1988).

Simnikiwe Buhlungu is an artist. Interested in knowledge production – how it is produced, by whom and how it is disseminated – Buhlungu locates socio-historical and everyday phenomena by navigating these questions and their inexhaustible potential answers via research-based methodologies. Through this, she maps points of cognisance which situate various layers of awareness as reverberated ecologies.

Omar Berrada is a writer and curator. His work focuses on the politics of translation and intergenerational transmission. He is the author of the poetry collection *Clonal Hum* and is currently researching racial dynamics in North Africa.

Taoufiq Izeddiou is a choreographer. He studied architecture before turning to dance. He founded the Anania Company, the first contemporary dance company in Morocco, as well as the *On Marche* festival. Among his works is *Botéro en Orient* (2019).

Thiago de Paula Souza is a curator and educator. He was co-curator of the 38th Panorama of Brazilian Art at MAM São Paulo (2024), the exhibition *Some May Work as Symbols: Art Made in*

Brazil, 1950s–70s at Raven Row (London), the Nomadic Program at Vleeshal Center for Contemporary Art (Middelburg) between 2022 and 2023, *While We Are Embattled*, at Para Site, Hong Kong), and *Atos de Revolta* (MAM Rio) in 2022. Between 2020 and 2021, he was part of the curatorial team for the 3rd edition of *Frestas* – Trienal de Artes (São Paulo). He served as curatorial advisor for the 58th Carnegie International (2021-2022). From 2018 to 2019, he curated Tony Cokes' first solo exhibition at BAK (Utrecht). He was also part of the curatorial team of the 10th Berlin Biennale (2018). He is currently a member of the Artistic Committee of the NESR Art Foundation in Angola and is a PhD candidate in the arts program at HDK-Valand – University of Gothenburg.

168

Bienal Archive
Leno Veras – *manager*
Antonio Paulo Carretta –
 coordinator
Marcele Souto Yakabi – *coordinator*
Ana Helena Grizotto Custódio
Anna Beatriz Corrêa Bortoletto
Daniel Malva Ribeiro
Gislene Sales
Gustavo Paes
Kleber Costa Timoteo
Raquel Coelho Moliterno
Thais Ferreira Dias
Alex Reimann – *intern*
Deisy Yumi – *intern*
Eloisa Elena – *intern*
Fabio Silva – *intern*
Juliana Knobel – *intern*
Maíra Alves – *intern*
Ricardo Menezes – *intern*
Walter Rocha – *intern*

Financial and Administrative

Finances
Amarildo Firmino Gomes –
 manager
Edson Pereira de Carvalho –
 coordinator
Fábio Kato
Silvia Andrade Simões Branco

Human Resources
Andréa Moreira – *human resources
 coordinator*
Higor Tocchio – *payroll and
 personnel department coordinator*
Matheus Andrade Sartori
Patricia Fernandes

Information Technology
Ricardo Bellucci
Jhones Alves do Nascimento
Júlio Coelho
Matheus Lourenço

Materials and Property
Valdomiro Rodrigues da Silva
 Neto – *manager*
Larissa Di Ciero Ferradas –
 coordinator
Angélica de Oliveira Divino
Daniel Pereira
Isabela Cardoso
Sergio Faria Lima
Victor Senciel
Vinícius Robson da Silva Araújo
Wagner Pereira de Andrade
Lucas Galhardo – *apprentice*

Planning and Operations
Rone Amabile
Vera Lucia Kogan

36ª Bienal de São Paulo – *Not All Travellers Walk Roads – Of Humanity as Practice*

Conceptual Team
Bonaventure Soh Bejeng Ndikung – *chief curator*
Alya Sebti, Anna Roberta Goetz, Thiago de Paula Souza – *co-curators*
Keyna Eleison – *co-curator at large*
Henriette Gallus – *strategy and communications advisor*
André Pitol, Leonardo Matsuhei – *curatorial assistance*

Architecture and Exhibition Design
Gisele de Paula, Tiago Guimarães – *architecture*
Alexandra Souza, Santiago Rid – *architectural assistance*
Agence Clémence Farrell – *initial architecture advisory*

Visual Identity
Studio Yukiko

AV Content and Photographic Documentation
Bruno Fernandes
Duma Hub de Inovação Criativa e Produção Artística
João Gabriel Hidalgo

Design
Aninha de Carvalho Price – *design assistance*
Tamara Lichtenstein – *design assistance*

Editorial
Cristina Fino – *editorial coordination of the educational publications #3 / #4*
Deborah Moreira – *editorial assistance*

Press Office
Index – *national press office*
Sam Talbot – *international press office*

Website
Fluxo

Invocations

Marrakech – Nov 14-15, 2024

LE 18 – co-convener
Laila Hida – *partner venue direction*
Youssef Sebti – *local production*
Zora El Hajji – *local press office*
Mahacine Mokdad, Sofian Amly, Hamza Morchid, Youssef Boumbarek – *AV content and photographic documentation*
Embaixada do Brasil em Rabat / Instituto Guimarães Rosa – Ministério das Relações Exteriores – *local support*

Guadeloupe – Dec 5-7, 2024

Lafabri'K – *co-convener*
Marie-Laure Poitout – *partner
 venue presidency*
Léna Blou – *partner venue direction*
Hellen Rugard – *local production*
Annik Benjamin – *simultaneous
 translation*
Cédric Marcellin, Philippe Hurgon –
 *AV content and photographic
 documentation*
Institut Français; Embaixada do
 Brasil em Paris / Instituto
 Guimarães Rosa – Ministério das
 Relações Exteriores – *local support*

Zanzibar – Feb 11-13, 2025

Bernard Ntahondi – *co-convener*
Dhow Countries Music Academy
 (DCMA) – *partner institution*
Halda Alkanaan – *partner institu-
 tion direction*
Thureiya Saleh – *local production*
Raymond Peter, Alex Marcel –
 sound engineering
William Chazega Nkobi,
 Habibu Ramadhani Diliwa – *simul-
 taneous translation*
Aden Rajab Said, Ally Nassor, Arafat
 Khamis Moh'd, Caroline-Jamie
 Dandu, Gulaam Abdullah, Venance
 Leonard, Waleed Khamis
 Mohammed – *AV content and
 photographic documentation*
YAS, Fondation H, Embaixada do
 Brasil em Dar es Salaam / Instituto
 Guimarães Rosa – Ministério das
 Relações Exteriores –
 local support

173

Tokyo – Apr 12-14, 2025

Andrew Maerkle, Kanako
 Sugiyama – *co-convener*
The 5th Floor; Sogetsu Kaikan;
 The University of Tokyo (with
 ACUT) – *venues*
Jordan A. Y. Smith – *poetry
 program advising*
Tomoya Iwata – *local production*
Yoshiko Kurata – *local press office*
Wataru Shoji – *sound engineering*
Art Translators Collective – *simulta-
 neous translation*
Kenji Agata, Naoki Takehisa, Sora
 Shirai, Takuma Osugi, Yoshikatsu
 Hirayama – *AV content and photo-
 graphic documentation*
Embaixada do Brasil em Tóquio /
 Instituto Guimarães Rosa –
 Ministério das Relações Exteriores;
 Art Center, The University of
 Tokyo (ACUT) – *local support*

Educational Publication #1

Edited by
Conceptual team and Fundação
 Bienal de São Paulo

Published by
Fundação Bienal de São Paulo and
 Center for Art, Research and
 Alliances (CARA), in Portuguese
 and English

Design
Studio Yukiko

**Editorial coordination, layout and
graphic production**
Fundação Bienal de São Paulo

Editorial assistance
Deborah Moreira

Copyediting and proofreading
Bruno Rodrigues, Guilherme Ziggy,
 Richard Sanches, Sandra Brazil

Translation
Andréia Manfrin, Cristina Fino,
 Jéssica Alonso, Mariana Nacif
 Mendes, Philip Somervell,
 Sergio Maciel

Font families
Arizona and Camera Plain
 by Dinamo

Printing
Ipsis

ISBN
978-1-954939-11-0

Distributed worldwide by
ARTBOOK | D.A.P.
75 Broad Street, Suite 630
New York, NY 10004
orders@dapinc.com
www.artbook.com

Fundação Bienal de São Paulo
Av. Pedro Álvares Cabral – Moema
04094-050 / São Paulo – SP
bienal.org.br

Center for Art, Research and Alliances (CARA)
225 West 13th Street,
New York, NY 10011
cara-nyc.org

Cataloging in Publication (CIP)

Souffles: On Deep Listening and Active Reception:
    educational publication: vol. 1 /
    edited by Fundação Bienal de São Paulo;
    curated by Bonaventure Soh Bejeng Ndikung. -- São Paulo:
    Bienal de São Paulo, 2025.

ISBN 978-1-954939-11-0

1. Art – São Paulo (State) – Exhibitions
2. Bienal de São Paulo (SP)
3. Culture
4. Education
5. Mediation

I. Fundação Bienal de São Paulo.
II. Ndikung, Bonaventure Soh Bejeng.

25-273124   CDD-709.8161

Systematic Catalog Index:
Art Biennials: São Paulo: City 709.8161

Antonio Paulo Carretta – Librarian – CRB-8/6084

Notes

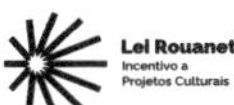
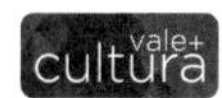
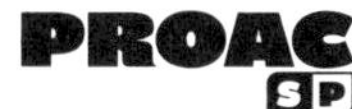

STRATEGIC PARTNERSHIP

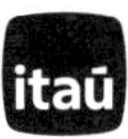

MASTER SPONSORSHIP

Bloomberg   bradesco   BR PETROBRAS   INSTITUTO CULTURAL VALE   citi   vivo

SPONSORSHIP

motiva   Alupar   ROLEX   ultra   [B]³   Lhoist

OSKLEN   CSN   CHANDON   comgás   MATTOS FILHO   UBS

IGUATEMI SÃO PAULO   Klabin   Unipar   J.Macêdo   OliverWyman   AGEO

COMOLATTI   AUTOMOB   sabesp   BANCO ABC BRASIL   VERDE asset management   biolab FARMACÊUTICA

OFFICIAL CARRIER   OFFICIAL AGENCY   SUPPORT

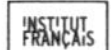
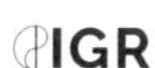
Creative   IOCHPE-MAXION   BR Partners   Banco Safra   PINHEIRO NETO ADVOGADOS

CULTURAL PARTNERSHIP

Instituto Rodobens   Toledo do Brasil Indústria de Balanças Ltda.   CHOCOLAT DU JOUR   instituto VOTORANTIM   BAHIA ASSET MANAGEMENT   J.P.Morgan   J.P.Morgan   sesc

INTERNATIONAL SUPPORT

INSTITUT FRANÇAIS   IGR   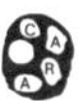   AaL BERG FOUNDATION   TAF Tanoto Art Foundation   National Center for Art Research, Japan   OCA Office for Contemporary Art Norway

LOCAL SUPPORT   LOCAL PARTNERSHIP

Yas   Canada Council for the Arts / Conseil des arts du Canada   ARTS COUNCIL NEW ZEALAND TOI AOTEAROA creative nz   EMBASSY OF BRAZIL RABAT   LE 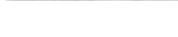   

INSTITUTIONAL SUPPORT   REALIZATION

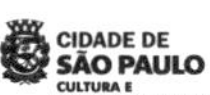
CIDADE DE SÃO PAULO CULTURA E ECONOMIA CRIATIVA   bienal são paulo   CULT SP   SP SÃO PAULO GOVERNO DO ESTADO — SÃO PAULO SÃO TODOS — Secretaria da Cultura, Economia e Indústria Criativas   MINISTÉRIO DAS RELAÇÕES EXTERIORES   MINISTÉRIO DA CULTURA   GOVERNO FEDERAL BRASIL UNIÃO E RECONSTRUÇÃO

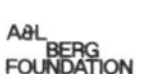
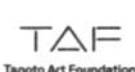
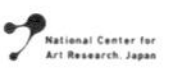
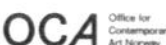
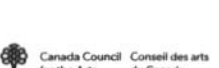
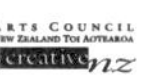
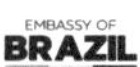
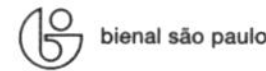
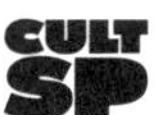
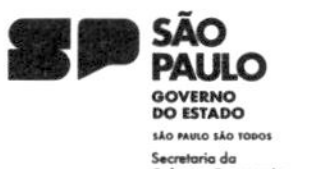
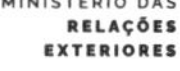
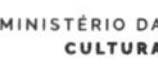
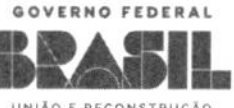